AF600514

THE CATHOLIC UNIVERSITY OF AMERICA
CANON LAW STUDIES
No. 320

THE JURISDICTION OF THE INTERRITUAL CONFESSOR IN THE UNITED STATES AND CANADA

BY THE

REV. JOHN J. WALSH, C.S.Sp., A.B., S.T.B., J.C.L.
Priest of the United States Province

A DISSERTATION

Submitted to the Faculty of the School of Canon Law of the Catholic University of America in Partial Fulfillment of the Requirements for the Degree of Doctor of Canon Law

THE CATHOLIC UNIVERSITY OF AMERICA PRESS
WASHINGTON, D. C.
1950

Imprimi Potest:

FRANCISCUS H. MCGLYNN, C.S.SP., S.T.D.,

Praepositus Provincialis.

Washingtonii, D. C., die 30 septembris 1950.

Nihil Obstat:

CLEMENS V. BASTNAGEL, J.U.D., S.T.L.,

Censor Deputatus.

Washingtonii, D. C., die 30 septembris 1950.

Imprimatur:

HENRICUS J. O'BRIEN, D.D.,

Episcopus Hartfordiensis.

Hartfordiae, die 2 octobris 1950.

Printed by

THE PAULIST PRESS

NEW YORK 19, N. Y.

51

TO

GOD THE HOLY GHOST

"Qui diceris Paraclitus,
Altissimi donum Dei,
Fons vivus, ignis, caritas,
Et spiritalis unctio."

TABLE OF CONTENTS

PAGE

FOREWORD vii

CHAPTER I

ECCLESIASTICAL JURISDICTION 1

ARTICLE 1. In the Universal Church 1

ARTICLE 2. In the United States and Canada 10

CHAPTER II

THE INTERRITUAL ADMINISTRATION OF THE SACRAMENT OF PENANCE 17

ARTICLE 1. Prior to the Promulgation of the Latin Code 17

A. Legislation of the IV Lateran Council (1215) 17

B. The Papal Confessional Privileges of Religious 22

C. Legislation from the Council of Trent to the Code 25

ARTICLE 2. The Law of the Latin Code 28

A. The Interritual Right of the Confessor 28

B. The Interritual Right of the Penitent 31

CHAPTER III

THE INTERRITUAL CONFESSOR WITH LOCAL JURISDICTION 35

ARTICLE 1. The Law of the Latin Code 35

ARTICLE 2. Confessors Subject to Local Ordinaries of the Latin Rite 42

A. Confessors of the Latin Rite 42

B. Confessors of the Oriental Rites 45

ARTICLE 3. Confessors Subject to Ruthenian Ordinaries 48

CHAPTER IV

PAGE

THE INTERRITUAL CONFESSOR WITH PERSONAL JURISDICTION 53
ARTICLE 1. Ordinary Personal Jurisdiction 55
ARTICLE 2. Delegated Personal Jurisdiction 59
A. From the Physical Person of the Delegator........ 59
B. From Positive Dispositions of the Law........ 63

CHAPTER V

THE MATERIAL COMPETENCE OF THE INTERRITUAL CONFESSOR 70
ARTICLE 1. Limitation of Material Competence........ 71
A. The Nature of Reservation 71
B. The Reservation to Which the Interritual Penitent Is Subject 74
1. Penitents of the Latin Rite........ 74
2. Penitents of the Oriental Rites........ 75
a. The Law of the Rite........ 75
b. The Law in the Territory........ 76
c. The Law in the Latin Code........ 76
C. The Interritual Confessor's Power to Absolve........ 84
1. Reservations of Local Ordinaries........ 84
2. Reservations of the Holy See........ 90
ARTICLE 2. Extension of Material Competence........ 95
CONCLUSIONS 103
BIBLIOGRAPHY 107
ABBREVIATIONS 114
ALPHABETICAL INDEX 115
BIOGRAPHICAL NOTE 119
CANON LAW STUDIES 121

FOREWORD

THE Church in the United States and Canada is predominantly Latin. To a certain extent however the various Oriental rites are represented among the residents of these countries. In many sections Latins and Orientals live side by side in the same town, city, parish or diocese. Now the Latin Code contains interritual canons which touch upon the relations between confessors and penitents who belong to canonically distinct rites. For example, canon 905 states that the faithful have the right to confess their sins to any duly authorized confessor even though he belongs to a rite other than their own. Canon 881, § 1, gives local confessors of the Latin rite explicit approval to administer the sacrament of penance to any penitent of the Oriental rites who approaches their local tribunal. These two factors, namely, the simultaneous presence of Latins and Orientals in the United States and Canada and the existence of the interritual laws on the sacrament of penance, are the occasion for the present work.

Any priest of the Latin or of an Oriental rite who hears the confession of a penitent who belongs to a rite other than his own is an interritual confessor. Any priest in the United States or Canada may occasionally be called upon to act as an interritual confessor. Such a priest may find himself confronted with possibly perplexing problems concerning the extent of his local, personal or material competence. Although much has been written about the confessor, comparatively few pages can be found which specifically discuss the interritual confessor or the extent of his jurisdictional power. The present study therefore aims to furnish information which may prove useful to the interritual confessor, especially in the United States and Canada, in solving at least some of his canonical problems.

The first chapter treats of ecclesiastical jurisdiction as it exists in the Church in general and in the United States and Canada in particular. The second chapter discusses the interritual administration of the sacrament of penance in accordance with the ecclesiastical legislation prior to and after the promulgation of the Latin Code.

The insertion of these two chapters, which are of an introductory character, was judged necessary before the more specific questions relative to the interritual confessor's jurisdiction could be properly discussed. The final three chapters discuss the specific extent of the interritual confessor's local, personal and material jurisdictional power.

The writer wishes to express his gratitude to the superiors of the United States Province of the Congregation of the Holy Ghost and of the Immaculate Heart of Mary for the opportunity of pursuing graduate studies in canon law; to the members of the faculty of the School of Canon Law of the Catholic University of America for their kind assistance and helpful direction; and to the many relatives and friends who by their prayers, interest and encouragement have made the completion of this dissertation possible.

CHAPTER I

ECCLESIASTICAL JURISDICTION

ARTICLE 1. IN THE UNIVERSAL CHURCH

THE Church founded by Christ is a juridically perfect, supernatural society whose end is the sanctification and the eternal salvation of its members.[1] Other definite and certain truths necessarily follow from this fundamental and basic doctrine. The very nature of a juridically perfect society postulates that it possess the means required to attain its end.

The constitutional nature of the Church, the unique supernatural, perfect society in the world, likewise demands that it possess the means proportionately necessary to accomplish the end determined and envisioned by its divine Founder. It must have the authoritative power to enable it to lead men to their eternal salvation. It must possess a complete juridical organization embracing the threefold power of rule.[2] As a matter of fact anyone who would dare say that the Church does not possess legislative, judicial and coactive power would be guilty of heretical doctrine.[3]

[1] Pius XI, litt. encycl. *Divini illius magistri,* 3 dec. 1929—*Acta Apostolicae Sedis, Commentarium Officiale* (Romae, 1909 . . .), XXII (1930), 52-53 (hereafter cited *AAS*).

[2] Cf. Billot, *Tractatus de Ecclesia Christi* (2 vols., Vol. I, *De Credibilitate Ecclesiae et de Intima Eius Constitutione,* 5 ed., Romae: Apud Aedes Universitatis Gregorianae, 1927), I, 450-466 (hereafter cited *De Ecclesia*).

[3] Pius VI, const. *Auctorem fidei,* 28 aug. 1794, prop. 5, Synodi Pistorien., damn.: "Qua parte insinuat, Ecclesiam non habere auctoritatem subiectionis suis decretis exigendae aliter quam per media, quae pendent a persuasione; quatenus intendat, Ecclesiam *non habere collatam sibi a Deo potestatem, non solum dirigendi per consilia et suasiones, sed etiam iubendi per leges, ac devios contumacesque exteriores iudicio ac salubribus poenis coercendi atque cogendi:*— inducens in systema alias damnatum ut haereticum." *Codicis Iuris Canonici Fontes, cura Emi. Petri Card. Gasparri editi,* (9 vols., Romae [postea Civitate Vaticana]: Typis Polyglottis Vaticanis, 1923-1939. Vols. VII-IX, ed. cura et studio Emi. Iustiniani Card. Serédi), n. 475 (hereafter cited *Fontes.*)

This public power to rule and to guide the faithful to their eternal salvation is one of the essential and treasured possessions of the Spouse of Christ. It is called ecclesiastical jurisdiction.[4] The source of ecclesiastical jurisdiction is divine, for it is inherent in the Church by reason of the latter's divine foundation.[5] Accordingly, for its origin it does not depend on the will of the faithful.[6] Since ecclesiastical jurisdiction is a property of a supreme, supernatural perfect society it is superior to the jurisdictional power of all other perfect societies. Consequently it should be respected and in no way limited by other perfect societies.

The Church's spiritual nature and supernatural end demand that its jurisdictional power be necessarily more extensive than that of other perfect societies. The material object of ecclesiastical jurisdiction is quite comprehensive, for "whatever in things human is of a sacred character, whatever belongs, either of its own nature or by reason of the end to which it is referred, to the salvation of souls, or to the worship of God, is subject to the power and judgment of the Church." [7]

Furthermore, the Church must have in view not only the public good of the society but also the individual sanctification of its members. Its jurisdictional power must extend, therefore, to the individual member's moral relations to God as well as to his social relations to the Church as a visible society. Ecclesiastical jurisdiction must embrace and extend to the internal forum of conscience as well as to the external or social forum. It is only in this way that the Church can efficaciously attain the end envisioned by Christ, its Founder.[8]

[4] Reiffenstuel, *Ius Canonicum Universum* (ed. R. D. Victoris Pelletier, 7 vols., Parisiis, 1864-1870), Lib. I, tit. XXIX, nn. 1-6; Ottaviani, *Institutiones Iuris Publici Ecclesiastici* (2 vols. in I, Romae: Apud Aedes Facultatis Iuridicae ad S. Apollinaris, 1925), n. 112 (hereafter cited *Institutiones*).

[5] Canon 196.

[6] Pius VI, *ibidem,* prop. 2 Synodi Pistorien. damn.

[7] Leo XIII, litt. encycl. *Immortale Dei,* 1 nov. 1885—*Fontes,* n. 592.

[8] Ottaviani, *op. cit.,* n. 120; Billot, *op. cit.,* I, 466-476; Gerald Ryan, *Principles of Episcopal Jurisdiction,* The Catholic University of America Canon Law Studies, n. 120 (Washington, D. C.: The Catholic University of America Press, 1939), p. 6.

Ecclesiastical jurisdiction of the external forum differs from that of the internal forum because each has a distinct material object and immediate end. The social actions of the members in their relation to the visible society are the material object of the external forum, whereas the moral actions of the individual member in their relation to God constitute the material object of the internal forum. The immediate end and purpose of jurisdiction of the external forum is the public good of the whole body; that of jurisdiction of the internal forum is the private good of the individual.[8a]

When the Church publicly regulates and judges the social actions of the faithful for the common good of the whole visible society, it exercises ecclesiastical jurisdiction in the external forum. When on the other hand it privately directs and judges the individual member's moral actions in their relation to God for the private and immediate benefit of the individual, it exercises ecclesiastical jurisdiction in the internal forum or in the forum of conscience. It is in virtue of ecclesiastical jurisdiction of the external forum that the faithful are found to be just or unjust, innocent or guilty in the eyes of the whole Church; it is in virtue of the Church's jurisdiction of the internal forum that they are found to be just or unjust, innocent or guilty, in the eyes of God.[9] When the latter type of jurisdiction is exercised within the sacred tribunal of the sacrament of penance it is called sacramental; when it is exercised apart from that tribunal it is said to be extra-sacramental.[10]

All ecclesiastical jurisdiction by reason of the title on which it is based is either ordinary or delegated. The former is that which by the law is attached to an office; the latter is that which is committed to a person.[11] Ordinary jurisdiction may be proper or vicarious.[12] Ordinary jurisdiction which is exercised in one's own name is proper, whereas that which is exercised by someone in the name

[8a] Ottaviani, *Institutiones,* n. 112.

[9] Beste, *Introductio in Codicem* (2. ed., Collegeville, Minn.: St. John's Abbey Press, 1944), p. 214 (hereafter cited *Introductio*).

[10] Canon 196.

[11] Canon 197, § 1.

[12] Canon 197, § 2.

of or as the representative of another is vicarious. Christ gave to His Church both these types of ordinary jurisdictional power.[13]

Every perfect society must have the necessary social power to enact and to enforce its laws, to pass judgment in contentious and in criminal cases, and to punish delinquents. Social power or jurisdiction of the external forum is proper to every perfect society precisely for the reason that it is a perfect society. Such power is proper to the Church because it is a perfect society. Consequently the Church exercises its social jurisdictional power of the external forum in its own name. Since the Church is also a supernatural society established by God to sanctify men, it exercises jurisdictional power in the internal forum of conscience. It exercises this latter power not in its own name, but rather in the name of God, to Whom exclusively the direct sanctification of men belongs. Canonists and theologians commonly teach therefore that the social jurisdictional power of the Church exists as a proper power, whereas that of the internal forum of conscience as a vicarious power.[14]

Ecclesiastical jurisdiction is not merely a potential treasure of the Holy, Catholic and Apostolic Church. It is rather a gift of God which is actually possessed and exercised by the incumbents of certain ecclesiastical offices or by their lawful delegates. Not all these ecclesiastical jurisdictional offices had the same origin. Some were established by Christ; others were instituted by the Church in the course of centuries. As a matter of fact there are only two divinely instituted jurisdictional offices in the Church, namely, the supreme pontificate and the subordinate episcopate.[15]

[13] Cf. Billot, *De Ecclesia,* I, 466-477.

[14] Cf. Billot, *op. cit.,* I, 466-467; Arturus Vermeersch et Josephus Creusen, *Epitome Iuris Canonici* (3 vols., I, 6. ed., 1937; Vol. II, 6. ed., 1940; Vol. III, 5. ed., 1936, Mechliniae: H. Dessain), I, n. 7 (hereafter cited *Epitome*); Michiels, *De Delictis et Poenis,* Vol. I, *De Delictis* (Lublin-Polonia: Universitas Catholica, 1934), p. 20 (hereafter cited *De Delictis*).

[15] Eugenius IV (in Conc. Florentin.) const. *Laetentur coeli,* 6 iul. 1439, n. 8—*Fontes,* n. 51; Conc. Vatican., sess. IV, c. 3—Denzinger-Bannwart-Umberg, *Enchiridion Symbolorum, Definitionum, et Declarationum de Rebus Fidei et Morum* (21-23. ed., Friburgi Brisgoviae: Herder & Co., 1937), n. 1826 (hereafter cited DB); Leo XIII, ep. encycl. *Satis cognitum,* 29 iun. 1896, §§ 13, 19—*Fontes,* n. 630; canons 108, § 3; 329, § 1; 218-219.

Christ built the Church on Peter, the Prince of the Apostles. In transmitting to Peter the power of the keys,[16] Christ gave him supreme jurisdictional power over the entire Church.[17] The primacy of Peter's power of jurisdiction was ordinary, official and communicable.[18] It was communicable because it was to be passed on to his successors in office. Thus the Roman Pontiff, the successor of St. Peter, by divine right actually possesses this unique, supreme, universal power of jurisdiction in the Church.[19] His power is truly episcopal, ordinary and immediate.[20]

A bishop either personally or through duly appointed clerics must administer the sacraments, make and enforce laws, visit his diocese, preach, settle controversies and judge and punish delinquents. In other words, all the functions which are necessary to lead the faithful to their eternal salvation fall within the scope of episcopal jurisdiction. The Bishop of Rome can perform all these functions throughout the whole world in virtue of his supreme episcopal jurisdiction.[21] His episcopal jurisdiction is truly ordinary, for by divine right it belongs to his office as Vicar of Christ on earth. It is immediate, for he can perform all the functions of his supreme episcopal office independently without the necessary intervention of any intermediary.[22] It would certainly be absurd for anyone to claim that the Roman Pontiff is obliged to ask the permission or consent of any subordinate bishop before administering confirmation or hearing the confessions of the faithful lawfully and validly.

This supreme jurisdictional power of the Bishop of Rome ex-

16 Matt., XVI:19.

17 Eugenius IV, *loc. cit.*; Leo XIII, *ibidem,* § 21.

18 Ryan, *Principles of Episcopal Jurisdiction,* p. 25.

19 Conc. Vatican., sess. IV, c. 3—DB, n. 1827; Gregorius XIII, a. 1575, Professio fidei Graecis praescr., § 5—*Fontes,* n. 146; canon 218, § 1.

20 Canon 218, § 2.

21 *Relatio de Emendatione cap. III Constitutionis Primae de Ecclesia Christi* (in Conc. Vatican.)—*Relatio R.P.D.F.M. Zinelli, Episcopi Tarvisini, Emendatio 14a—Acta et Decreta Sacrorum Conciliorum Recentiorum, Collectio Lacensis* (7 vols., Friburgi Brisgoviae, 1870-1892), VII, 351-352 (hereafter cited *Coll. Lac.*).

22 Cf. *Relatio R.P.D.F.M. Zinelli, Episcopi Tarvisini, Emendatio 14a—loc. cit.*

tends to every member of the Church, of whatever rite or dignity, throughout the world.[23] All, whether they belong to an Oriental or to the Latin rite, are equally subject to his jurisdiction in matters of faith, morals, government and discipline.[24] So extensive is his jurisdictional power that it knows no limits but those established by divine law. Consequently the Vicar of Christ can withhold or remove from the particular jurisdiction of bishops certain persons, certain places and certain affairs which would otherwise be subject to their jurisdiction.[25] By pontifical law these affairs which, by reason of their nature or of positive law, are reserved to the Roman Pontiff are called *causae maiores*.[26] The very nature of his office also demands that his jurisdiction embrace the internal forum of conscience as well as the external forum.[27]

This unique supreme jurisdiction of the Roman Pontiff does not destroy but rather strengthens the ordinary and immediate jurisdiction of the subordinate episcopate.[28] By reason of the divine institution of their episcopal office the bishops are the lawful successors of the apostles.[29] They do not succeed however to identically the same power as that which was enjoyed by the apostles. The main difference is that, whereas the jurisdictional episcopal power of the apostles was not limited to any particular place or persons, the power of bishops is juridically so limited.[30]

The episcopal power of bishops over the persons committed to their care is ordinary, proper and immediate.[31] This power, though

[23] Conc. Vatican., sess. IV, c. 3—DB, n. 1827.

[24] Benedictus XII, a. 1341, prop. 90, Armenorum, damn.—*Fontes,* n. 40; Eugenius IV (in Conc. Florentin.), const. *Laetentur coeli,* 6 iul. 1439, n. 8—*Fontes,* n. 51; Pius VI, const. *Auctorem fidei,* 28 aug. 1794, prop. 6, Synodi Pistorien., damn.—*Fontes,* n. 475; canon 218, § 1.

[25] Pius VI, *ibidem,* prop. 7, damn.—*Fontes,* n. 475; cf. also Billot, *De Ecclesia,* I, 713.

[26] Canon 220.

[27] Cf. Benedictus XIV, const. *Sacramentum poenitentiae,* 1 iun. 1741—*Codex Iuris Canonici,* Documentum V; canons 873 and 884.

[28] Conc. Vatican., sess. IV, c. 3—DB, n. 1826.

[29] Canon 329, § 1.

[30] Cf. *Principles of Episcopal Jurisdiction,* pp. 24-25.

[31] Leo XIII ep. encycl. *Satis cognitum,* 29 iun. 1896, n. 25—*Fontes,* n. 630.

divinely established, exists together with and in subordination to the supreme papal authority of the Roman Pontiff. It is essentially dependent upon the supreme power of the successor of St. Peter. As such it is necessarily limited to a certain territory, to certain persons or to certain affairs by the general or particular laws of the Church.[32] Within his particular competence, however, the bishop is in a sense supreme. He has the right to rule the subjects committed to his care with true legislative, judicial and coactive power.[33] His power, like that of the Roman Pontiff, extends within his competence to the internal as well as to the external forum. No patriarch, primate, metropolitan or other ecclesiastic, even though he enjoy similar episcopal jurisdiction, is entitled to assume the power that belongs to another except in accordance with the express provisions of law.[34]

Besides these two divinely established jurisdictional ecclesiastical offices the Church in the course of centuries has instituted many others both in the East and in the West for the purpose of more efficiently ruling the faithful divinely committed to its care. The jurisdictional power which the incumbents of the latter offices possess is a participation either of the supreme jurisdiction of the Roman Pontiff or of that of the subordinate episcopate. The Code lists the various jurisdictional offices of ecclesiastical origin as they exist in the present discipline of the Latin Church as well as the general laws which define the particular competence of each.[35]

It is a more difficult matter to determine the various offices as they exist in the present discipline of the various Oriental rites.

[32] Cf. Billot, *De Ecclesia,* I, 711-713.

[33] Canon 335, § 1; Signatura Ap., *Romana* (Iurium), 15 dec. 1923: "Haec Episcoporum potestas [canonis 335, § 1] nullos habet fines, nisi generales Ecclesiae leges et peculiaria Pontificum decreta. Idcirco quae neque per generales leges neque per peculiaria Pontificum decreta constituta sunt, ea Episcoporum subiacent potestati."—*AAS,* XVI (1924), 107.

[34] Conc. Constantinopolitan. I (381), canon 2—Mansi, *Sacrorum Conciliorum Nova et Amplissima Collectio* (53 vols. in 60, Parisiis, Arnhem, Lipsiae, 1901-1927), III, 559 (hereafter cited Mansi); Benedictus XIV, const. *Demandatam,* 24 dec. 1743, n. 12—*Fontes,* n. 338; const. *Inter multa,* 4 apr. 1747—*Fontes,* n. 379; F. X. Wernz, *Ius Decretalium* (6 vols., Vols. I-IV, 2. ed., Romae et Prati, 1905-1912), II, n. 713.

[35] Lib. II, Pars I, tit. VII-VIII.

This results from the fact that the complete Oriental Code of Canon Law has not as yet been promulgated. It must be noted however that there do exist in the Oriental Church some jurisdictional offices of ecclesiastical institution which are not found in the present discipline of the Latin Church. Thus, for example, in the Ruthenian rite there are Apostolic Exarchs; [36] in the Armenian Rite, *Chorepiscopi*,[37] and in the Maronite Rite, *Periodeutae*.[38]

In the Oriental rites as in the Latin rite there are ecclesiastical offices whose incumbents possess jurisdictional power which is simultaneously inferior to that of the Roman Pontiff and superior to that of the successors of the Apostles. In the universal Church there are metropolitans, whose jurisdictional power is superior to that of individual bishops; in some of the Oriental rites there are patriarchs, whose jurisdiction extends over all the metropolitans and bishops of their rite within the patriarchal territory.[39] The incumbents of such jurisdictional offices occupy an intermediate position in the hierarchy of jurisdiction in the Church.

By divine right all bishops are equal. Any gradation of jurisdictional power that may exist between them is necessarily accidental. No bishop has superior authority over another unless such authority has been given him by the Roman Pontiff.[40] The superior jurisdiction of metropolitans and primates in the universal Church and of patriarchs in the Oriental Church is therefore fundamentally a participation in the supreme jurisdictional power of the

[36] *Annuario Pontificio per l'anno 1948* (Città del Vaticano: Tipographia Poliglotta Vaticana, 1948), pp. 599-600 (hereafter cited *Annuario Pontificio (1948)*.

[37] *Acta et Decreta Concilii Nationis Armenorum Romae habiti, an. 1911* (Romae: Typis Polyglottis Vaticanis, 1913), n. 301.

[38] *Codificazione Canonica Orientale, Fonti,* Serie I, Fasc. XII, *Disciplina Antiochena* (Maroniti): *Testi di diritto particolare dei Maroniti* (Romae: Typis Polyglottis Vaticanis, 1933), nn. 1168-1177 (hereafter cited *Fonti,* Serie I, Fasc. XII).

[39] Cf. *Fonti,* Serie I, Fasc. XII, nn. 1108-1166; Pius IX, litt. ap. *Reversurus,* 12 iul. 1867—*Fontes,* n. 546; Leo XIII, litt. ap. *Orientalium,* 30 nov. 1894, n. XIII—*Fontes,* n. 627.

[40] Pius IX, litt. ap. *Reversurus,* 12 iul. 1867—*Fontes,* n. 546; Wernz, *Ius Decretalium,* II, n. 713.

Roman Pontiff.[41] It would be wrong to conclude that the jurisdiction which is possessed by the incumbents of these ecclesiastical offices is of a delegated character simply for the reason that it is derived from the supreme power of the Bishop of Rome. It is not delegated but ordinary power, for it is attached by common or particular law to the office. By the very fact that one becomes an incumbent of one of these offices one automatically possesses the jurisdiction which is attached to that office.

Although many prelates of the Latin rite bear the title of patriarch,[42] that title ordinarily[43] does not carry with it any power of jurisdiction.[44] The same cannot be said of the reigning patriarchs of the various Oriental rites,[45] for they actually possess jurisdiction over all the clergy and faithful of their rite who have been committed to their care.[46] Their jurisdiction does not however extend beyond their patriarchal territory.[47] They are nevertheless obliged to communicate to the members of their rite living outside the patriarchate all the regulations which pertain to the liturgy and to the rite as such.[48] The purpose of communicating the regulations *quoad ritum tantum* to the members of the rite who are living outside the patriarchal territory is the preservation of the purity and of the uniformity of the particular Oriental rite.[49]

41 Wernz, *loc. cit.*

42 Cf. *Annuario Pontificio (1948)*, pp. 84-87.

43 The one notable exception is the Latin Patriarch of Jerusalem. Cf. *Annuario Pontificio (1948)*, p. 85.

44 Canon 271.

45 Cf. *Annuario Pontificio (1948)*, pp. 84-87.

46 Pius IX, litt. ap. *Reversurus*, 12 iul. 1867, n. 11—*Fontes*, n. 546; *Synodus Sciarfensis Syrorum in Monte Libano celebrata, an. 1888* (Romae: Typis Polyglottis S. C. de Prop. Fide, 1896), p. 217 (hereafter cited *Synodus Sciarfensis*); Leo XIII, litt. ap. *Orientalium*, 30 nov. 1894, n. XIII—*Fontes*, n. 627.

47 Leo XIII, *ibid.*, n. IX.

48 Cf. Diederichs, *The Jurisdiction of the Latin Ordinaries over Their Oriental Subjects*, The Catholic University of America Canon Law Studies, n. 229 (Washington, D. C.: The Catholic University of America Press, 1946), p. 45.

49 Coussa, *Epitome Praelectionum de Iure Ecclesiastico Orientali* (2 vols., Vol. I, Romae: Typis Polyglottis Vaticanis, 1940), n. 135 (hereafter cited *Epitome*); Diederichs, *op. cit.*, pp. 45-46.

Thus it is that the Church exercises its power of jurisdiction over the members of the Latin and Oriental rites through competent officers chosen according to the prescriptions of general or particular law. Each officer, within the scope of his particular competence directs and guides the faithful committed to his care. The Roman Pontiff exercises supreme, universal and independent jurisdiction over the entire Church; the patriarch rules the clergy and the faithful of his rite within his patriarchal boundaries; the metropolitan makes use of the jurisdiction of his metropolitan office within his ecclesiastical province; the bishop rules the flock committed to his care; the pastor possesses certain ordinary powers of jurisdiction which enable him to assist the subordinate episcopate in guiding souls toward their eternal salvation.

Article 2. In the United States and Canada

The territory of the United States and Canada is divided into provinces and dioceses. Each has its own metropolitan or bishop. Each bishop rules his diocese with full episcopal jurisdiction.[50] Before the twentieth century all the metropolitans and bishops were of the Latin rite. Within their territorial boundaries they ruled all the faithful subject to their jurisdiction irrespective of the rite to which the latter belonged. With the erection of the Ruthenian jurisdictions the twentieth century witnessed a slight modification in the previous jurisdictional constitution of the Church in the United States and Canada.

Until the middle of the nineteenth century the Church in North America was not confronted with any interritual problem. The reason was that until this time practically all the Catholics in this territory belonged to the Latin rite. The latter half of the nineteenth century, however, witnessed a great influx of immigrants from Eastern Europe and the Near East, who came to settle in the new land of freedom, of progress and of opportunity. Represented in the great immigration movement were Catholics who belonged to the various Oriental disciplines and rites. Groups of Catholics of the following rites were soon settled in the United

[50] Canons 329, § 1, and 335.

States or Canada: Armenian, Chaldean, Pure Syrian, Maronite, Melkite, Ruthenian, Rumanian, Italo-Greek and Russian.[51]

Quite naturally the larger groups wanted priests of their own rite to minister to their spiritual needs. Oriental priests soon arrived in answer to the urgent demands of the faithful of their rite. Unfortunately some of these priests refused to submit to the jurisdiction of the local Latin ordinaries. The advent of the Oriental Catholics indeed created new problems for the local Latin hierarchy.

The American hierarchy had recourse to the Holy See. On October 1, 1890, the Sacred Congregation for the Propagation of the Faith issued an encyclical letter which contained the following regulations for all priests of the Greek Ruthenian rite who desired to exercise the sacred ministry in the United States: (1) They must be celibates; (2) they must receive their faculties from the ordinary of the place where they desire to exercise the sacred ministry, and (3) they must be subject to the episcopal jurisdiction of the local ordinary.[52] A few years later these regulations were extended to the priests of all the Oriental rites who desired to exercise the sacred ministry in the United States.[53]

Pope Leo XIII (1878-1903) issued his celebrated Apostolic Letter *Orientalium* on November 30, 1894. In this letter he re-

[51] Cf. Pallen, *A Memorial of Andrew J. Shipman, His Life and Writings* (New York: Encyclopedia Press, Inc., 1916), pp. 83-121, 155-239; Marbach, *Marriage Legislation for the Catholics of the Oriental Rites in the United States and Canada,* The Catholic University of America Canon Law Studies, n. 243 (Washington, D. C.: The Catholic University of America Press, 1946), pp. 141-203; Bélanger, *Les Ukrainiens catholiques du rit grec-ruthène au Canada* (Québec: L'Université Laval, 1945), pp. 7-8; Diederichs, *op. cit.,* pp. 28-40; Duskie, *The Canonical Status of Orientals in the United States,* The Catholic University of America Canon Law Studies, n. 48 (Washington, D. C.: The Catholic University of America, 1928), p. 30.

[52] *Collectanea S. Congregationis de Propaganda Fide* (2 vols., Romae, 1907), n. 1966, nota 2 (hereafter cited *Coll. S.C.P.F.*).

[53] S. C. de Prop. Fide, decr., 10 maii 1892—*The American Ecclesiastical Review* (Vols. I-XXXII, Philadelphia, 1889-1905; from 1905: *The Ecclesiastical Review,* Vols. XXXIII-CIX, Philadelphia, 1905-1943; from 1944: *The American Ecclesiastical Review,* Washington, D. C., Vol. CX, 1944—), VII, (1892), 66-67 (hereafter cited *AER* and *ER* respectively).

peated the general principle that all the faithful of the Oriental rites who were living outside their own patriarchate or Oriental territory must be subject to the jurisdiction of the local Latin ordinary.[54] On May 1, 1897, the Holy See explicitly extended the regulations previously made for the faithful and clergy of the Oriental rites in the United States to all Oriental Catholics who were living in North America.[55] These general provisions with later modifications [56] still retain their legislative force for all the priests and the faithful of the Oriental rites in North America except for those of the Greek Ruthenian rite.

In view of the large numbers of Ruthenian Catholics in the United States, Pope Pius X (1903-1914) acceded to their request by creating a titular bishop of the Ruthenian rite in 1907.[57] The titular Ruthenian bishop was to rule the faithful of his rite in the United States as the vicar of the local Latin ordinaries. He had no ordinary power of jurisdiction, but received delegated power from the Latin ordinary of each diocese in which he desired to exercise his sacred ministry.[58] This arrangement did not prove satisfactory, for the titular bishop was soon given full, ordinary, episcopal jurisdiction over all the members of his rite in the United States.[59] To clarify the juridic status of the new Ruthenian ordinariate, the Holy See issued a decree on August 17, 1914, entitled *Cum Episcopo,* which was to be in force for ten years.[60]

The Holy See divided the Ruthenian jurisdiction in the United

[54] N. IX—*Fontes,* n. 627.

[55] S. C. de Prop. Fide, decr.—*Fontes,* n. 4935.

[56] Cf. S. C. Or., decr. *Qua sollerti,* 23 dec. 1929—*AAS,* XXII (1930), 99-105; Bouscaren, *The Canon Law Digest* (2 vols. and Supplement, Milwaukee: Bruce, 1934, 1943, 1949), I, 17-24 (hereafter cited *Digest*); decr. *Non raro accidit,* 7 ian. 1930—*AAS,* XXII (1930), 106-108; Bouscaren, *Digest,* I, 24-26; instr., 26 sept. 1932—*AAS,* XXIV (1932), 334-346; Bouscaren, *ibidem,* 39-42.

[57] Litt. ap. *Ea semper,* 12 maii 1907—*Acta Sanctae Sedis,* (41 vols., Romae, 1865-1908), XLI (1908), 3-12 (hereafter cited *ASS*).

[58] Pius X, *ibid.,* art. 2.

[59] S. C. de Prop. Fide, decr. *Cum Episcopo,* 17 aug. 1914—*AAS,* VI (1914), 458-463.

[60] S. C. de Prop. Fide, *loc. cit.;* cf. Meehan, *The Greek Ruthenian Church in the United States*—*ER,* LI (1914), 710-717.

States in 1924.[61] His Excellency, the Most Reverend Constantine Bohachevsky, was given episcopal jurisdiction over the Ruthenians whose national origin was Galicia, while His Excellency, the Most Reverend Basil Takach, received episcopal jurisdiction over the Ruthenians whose national origin was Russian Podcarpathia, Hungary and Jugoslavia.[62] Because of changing circumstances the former Decree *Cum Episcopo,* which had served as the particular law for the Ruthenians in the United States, was abrogated in 1929 and was replaced with a new decree entitled *Cum data fuerit.*[63] This latter decree, slightly modified and renewed for ten years in 1940,[64] still serves as the particular law for all Ruthenians in the United States.

In Canada the number of Ruthenians also increased to such an extent that the need of a Ruthenian ordinary was evident. On the occasion of the International Eucharistic Congress of Montreal in 1910 the bishops of Canada invited His Excellency the Most Reverend Andrew Szeptyskij, Archbishop of Lwow and Metropolitan of Galicia, to visit the Ruthenians in Canada. Upon seeing the large number of Ruthenians and after discussing the inter-ritual problems with the Canadian bishops, he recommended that the Holy See appoint a Ruthenian ordinary for Canada.[65] The Holy See acted upon this recommendation by appointing a Ruthenian ordinary to care for the faithful of the Ruthenian rite in Canada.[66]

The Decree *Fidelibus Ruthenis,* which was issued in 1913 and which was to serve as the particular law for the newly erected Ruthenian ordinariate, gave the Ruthenian bishop full, ordinary, episcopal jurisdiction over all the Catholics of the Ruthenian rite in Canada.[67] The Sacred Congregation for the Oriental Church in 1930 issued a new decree, *Graeci-Rutheni Ritus,* which sup-

[61] Cf. *AAS,* XVI (1924), 243.

[62] S. C. Or., decr. *Cum data fuerit,* 1 mart. 1929—*AAS,* XXI (1929), 152-159; Bouscaren, *Digest,* I, 6-16.

[63] S. C. Or., *loc. cit.*

[64] Cf. *AAS,* XXXIII (1941), 27; Bouscaren, *Digest,* II, 6-7.

[65] Bélanger, *Les Ukrainiens catholiques du rit grec-ruthène au Canada,* p. 17.

[66] S. C. de Prop. Fide, 12 iul. 1912—*AAS,* IV (1912), 531.

[67] S. C. de Prop. Fide, 18 aug. 1913—*AAS,* V (1913), 393-399.

planted the former one and still serves as the particular law for the Ruthenians in Canada.[68]

In 1948 Pope Pius XII, who has always been solicitous for and ever alert to promote the spiritual welfare of the members of the Oriental rites, divided the Ruthenian Exarchate of Canada into three: The Apostolic Exarchate of Central Canada, with its see in Winnipeg, The Apostolic Exarchate of Eastern Canada, with its see in Toronto, and The Apostolic Exarchate of Western Canada, with its see in Edmonton.[69] The basic consideration underlying the making of this division was territorial residence,[70] whereas the one underlying the dividing of the Ruthenian Ordinariate of the United States was national origin.[71] Consequently while the two Ruthenian exarchates in the United States are personally distinct but locally coterminous, the three Ruthenian exarchates in Canada are personally and locally distinct.

Thus at the present time in the United States and Canada there are two distinct jurisdictions, namely, the territorial jurisdiction of the residential bishops of the Latin rite and the personal-territorial jurisdiction[72] of the ordinaries of the Ruthenian rite. Although their jurisdictional power is substantially similar, it does not follow that it is identical. There are some important differences between the two jurisdictions. The jurisdiction of the residential bishops of the Latin rite is primarily territorial, whereas that of the Ruthenian ordinaries is primarily personal. The jurisdiction

[68] 24 maii 1930—*AAS,* XXII (1930), 346-354; Bouscaren, *Digest,* I, 29-39; Pius XII, const. *Omnium cuiusvis ritus,* 3 mart. 1948—*AAS,* XL (1948), 287-290.

[69] Const. *Omnium cuiusvis ritus,* 3 mart. 1948—*AAS,* XL (1948), 287-290.

[70] The Ruthenian Exarchate of Central Canada comprises the civil provinces of Manitoba and Saskatchewan and the regions North to the Arctic Ocean; that of Eastern Canada embraces the civil provinces of Ontario, Quebec, New Brunswick, Nova Scotia, Prince Edward Island, Newfoundland and Labrador; that of Western Canada extends over the territory of the civil provinces of Alberta and British Columbia, the Yukon and the regions North to the Arctic Ocean. Cf. Pius XII, *ibid.*—*AAS,* XL (1948), 287-288; *The Official Catholic Directory (1949),* (New York: P. J. Kenedy & Sons, 1949), Part III, pp. 117-120.

[71] Cf. *supra,* p. 13.

[72] Cf. *Annuario Pontificio (1948),* pp. 599-600.

of the latter is territorial in the sense that it is confined to the United States or to certain portions of Canada. Within these territorial boundaries it has further personal limitations, since it extends only to the clergy and to the faithful of the Ruthenian rite.[73] The residential bishops of the Latin rite can exercise their full episcopal jurisdiction over all non-Ruthenians within their respective dioceses.[74]

According to the *Annuario Pontificio* the Ruthenian ordinaries in North America are apostolic exarchs and titular bishops.[75] In the early days of the Church an exarch had extensive jurisdictional prerogatives in the East. The exarchs of Ephesus, Caesarea and Heraclea exercised jurisdiction over all the ecclesiastical provinces and eparchies of Asia, Pontus and Thrace respectively.[76] When the exarchs had lost their superior jurisdictional power, the name was still retained in the Oriental Church as a title of honor.[77]

The Ruthenian ordinaries in North America are probably given the title *exarch* because of the resemblance between the vast territorial extent of their jurisdictional power and that which was enjoyed by the exarchs in the early days of the Church. They are called *apostolic exarchs* in indication of their immediate subjection to the Holy See. The use of the word *apostolic* seems also to involve a further connotation relative to the nature of their jurisdiction. It seems that their episcopal jurisdictional power is exercised not in their own name but rather in the name of the Roman Pontiff. Thus they are not bishops of residential sees in this country; they are titular bishops.[78] Like the ordinary jurisdiction of

[73] Pius XII, const. *Omnium cuiusvis ritus*, 3 mart. 1948—*AAS*, XL (1948), 287-290; S. C. Or., decr. *Cum data fuerit*, 1 mart. 1929, art. 2, 19—*AAS*, XXI (1929), 152-159; Bouscaren, *Digest*, I, 6-16; *Graeci-Rutheni Ritus*, 24 maii 1930, art. 2, 21—*AAS*, XXII (1930), 346-354; Bouscaren, *op. cit.*, I, 29-39.

[74] Cf. *supra*, pp. 13-14.

[75] *Annuario Pontificio (1948)*, pp. 599-600.

[76] Cf. Thomassinus, *Vetus et Nova Ecclesiae Disciplina circa Benficia et Beneficiarios* (10 vols., Magontiaci, 1787), Pars I, lib. I, tit. 31, cap. 17 (hereafter cited Thomassinus); Wernz, *Ius Decretalium*, II, n. 717.

[77] Vermeersch-Creusen, *Epitome*, I, n. 388.

[78] Cf. *Annuario Pontificio (1948)*, pp. 599-600; *The Official Catholic Directory, (1949)*, Part II, pp. 601, 604; Part III, pp. 117-120.

vicars and of prefects apostolic,[79] the ordinary episcopal jurisdiction of the apostolic exarchs of the Ruthenian rite in North America is of a vicarious character. The ordinary jurisdiction of the residential bishops of the Latin rite on the contrary is not of a vicarious but of a proper stamp and character.[80]

The erection of the Ruthenian jurisdictions or exarchates also has real consequences. It removes all the clergy, the faithful, the missions, the parishes, the schools, the cemeteries, the associations and all things that belong to the Ruthenian Church in the United States and Canada from the jurisdiction and from the vigilance of the local ordinaries of the Latin rite.[81] Thus a personal and real dismemberment of the territorial dioceses has been effected. As a result the Ruthenian ordinaries have the exclusive right and power to rule and govern the flocks committed to their care. They have the right to establish laws and statutes concerning all the ecclesiastical affairs of the Ruthenian Church in this country, provided that they are not contrary to the existing common or particular law.[82]

[79] Vermeersch-Creusen, *op. cit.*, I, n. 404; Beste, *Introductio,* p. 215; Coronata, *Institutiones Iuris Canonici* (2. ed., 5 vols., Taurini-Romae: Marietti, 1939-1947), I, n. 279 (hereafter cited *Institutiones.*).

[80] Cf. *supra,* pp. 3-4.

[81] S. C. Or., decr. *Cum data fuerit,* 1 mart. 1929, art. 4, 6, 19, 37—*AAS,* XXI (1929), 152-159; Bouscaren, *Digest,* I, 6-16; *Graeci-Rutheni Ritus,* 24 maii 1930, art. 4, 6, 21, 43—*AAS,* XXII (1930), 346-354; Bouscaren, *op. cit.,* I, 29-39.

[82] S. C. Or., *decr. cit.,* art. 3.

CHAPTER II

THE INTERRITUAL ADMINISTRATION OF THE SACRAMENT OF PENANCE

Article 1. Prior to the Promulgation of the Latin Code

In the early Christian Church the presence in the same city or diocese of large groups of the faithful of different language, rite and customs was certainly not general. Probably in some of the large commercial centers of the East and West there were groups of Christian foreigners. In these centers, where the number of these Christians warranted it, arrangements were most probably made so that they could worship God and receive the sacraments according to their own rite and customs. It is known, for example, that there were Greek monasteries and churches in Rome, and Latin churches and monasteries in Constantinople, prior to the schism of Caerularius (1054).[1] In other localities where similar provisions had not been made, these Christian foreigners, in default of a priest of their own language and rite, followed the customs of the place where they happened to be.[2] They received the sacraments most probably according to the rite and customs of that particular place.

A. *Legislation of the IV Lateran Council* (1215).

In the thirteenth century the Church recognized the fact that the presence of Catholics of different language and rite within the

[1] Leo IX, ep. *In terra pax,* 2 sept. 1053—Mansi, XIX, 652; Jaffé, *Regesta Pontificum Romanorum ab condita Ecclesia ad annum post Christum natum MCXVIII* (2. ed. correctam et auctam auspiciis Gulielmi Wattenbach curaverunt S. Loewenfeld, F. Kaltenbrunner, P. Ewald, 2 tomes in 1 vol., Lipsiae, 1885-1888), n. 4302.

[2] S. Augustinus, ep. *Dilectissimo Januario*—". . . Ambrosius ait mihi: Cum Romam venio, jejuno sabbato; cum hic sum, non jejuno. Sic etiam tu, ad quam forte Ecclesiam veneris, eius morem serva, si cuiquam non vis esse scandalo, nec quemquam tibi."—Migne, *Patrologiae Cursus Completus, Series Latina* (221 vols., Parisiis, 1844-1864), XXXIII, 20 (hereafter cited *MPL*).

same city or diocese was not so exceptional a situation. The IV General Council of the Lateran (1215) found it necessary to enact legislation which made provisions for the proper spiritual care of the faithful of different language and rite who lived in the mixed diocese of the East and West. Canon IX of this council obliged the bishops of such mixed dioceses to provide suitable men to perform the various acts of divine worship, to preach the word of God and to administer the sacraments according to the rite and language of the faithful.[3] This law was binding on all ordinaries in union with Rome. It embraced Latins and Orientals, both in the East and in the West.[4]

The men thus provided according to the prescriptions of the law had to be suitable. To be considered suitable they had to be priests, for otherwise they neither could have preached nor could they have heard the confessions of the faithful confided to their care.[5] The law itself did not use the term *pastor* to designate the priest who had the care of the faithful of a particular language and rite. From the nature of his duties toward this group of the faithful the latter were certainly to be considered his parishioners. At any rate such a priest was their *proper* priest to whom many spiritual functions were reserved by the canons.[6]

The IV Lateran Council also enacted general legislation relative to the administration and the reception of the sacrament of penance. Canon XXI obliged all Catholics, after they had come to the use of reason, to confess their sins at least annually to their proper priest.[7]

[3] C. 14, X, *de officio iudicis ordinarii,* I, 31.

[4] *Fontes,* Series III, Vol. II, *Acta Innocentii PP. III* (1198-1216) (e registris vaticanis aliisque eruit, introductione auxit, notisque illustravit P. Theodosius Haluscynskyj, Città del Vaticano: Typis Polyglottis Vaticanis, 1944), pp. 477-485 (hereafter cited *Fontes,* Series III, Vol. II).

[5] Hostiensis, *In Libros Decretalium Commentaria* (5 vols. in 3, Venetiis, 1581), lib. 1, tit. XXXI, cap. 14, n. 1 (hereafter cited Hostiensis); Gonzalez-Tellez, *Commentaria Perpetua in Singulos Textus Quinque Librorum Decretalium Gregorii IX* (5 vols. in 4, Venetiis, 1699), lib. 1, tit. XXXI, cap. 14, n. 4 (hereafter cited Gonzalez-Tellez).

[6] Cf., e.g., c. 12, X, *de poenitentiis et remissionibus,* V, 38.

[7] "Omnis utriusque sexus fidelis, postquam ad annos discretionis pervenerit, omnia sua solus peccata saltem semel in anno fideliter confiteatur, proprio sacerdoti . . . Si quis autem alieno sacerdoti voluerit iusta de causa sua

If any of the faithful desired to go to confession to another priest, he was obliged to ask and to receive the permission of the priest or bishop to whose spiritual care he had been entrusted. Otherwise the absolution of another priest was illicit and invalid.[8]

This law on annual confession certainly bound all Latins, for by its inclusion in the Decretals of Gregory IX it became Decretal law with the promulgation of this collection in 1234.[9] Pope Innocent III (1198-1216) also extended the law to the Maronites, whose Patriarch, Jeremias, was in attendance at the Council.[10] Application of the law was also made in Cyprus by the National Council which was held at Nicosia toward the end of the thirteenth century.[11]

The only innovation contained in Canon XXI of the IV Lateran Council was the obligation which it imposed on the faithful of confessing their sins at least once a year. Otherwise it merely expressed the canonical teaching and common practice of the Western Church, according to which only such priests as were entrusted with the care of souls had ordinary jurisdiction to hear the confessions of their subjects.[12] Other priests could not grant valid sacramental absolution unless the bishop or the priest who had the care of souls gave them jurisdiction over his subjects.[13] As is clear, the law of annual confession to one's proper priest limited the freedom of both the confessor and the penitent in all those places where it had the binding force of law. The penitent was free to confess his sins only to

confiteri peccata, licentiam prius postulet et obtineat a proprio sacerdote, quum aliter ipse illum non possit absolvere vel ligare."—c. 12, X, *de poenitentiis et remissionibus,* V, 38.

8 *Loc. cit.*

9 Cf. *Codex Iuris Canonici, Praefatio,* XXII-XXIII.

10 Bulla ap. *Quia divinae sapientiae,* 4 ian. 1215—*Fontes,* Series III, Vol. II, pp. 459-460.

11 *Constitutio instruens Graecos et alios* (1278-1288), n. 7—Mansi, XXVI, 328.

12 Cf. c. 2, C. IX, q. 2; *Dictum* ad c. 19, C. XVI, q. 1; c. 3, D. VI, *de poenit.;* Bernardus Papiensis, *Summa Decretalium* (ed. E. A. Th. Laspeyres, Ratisbonae, 1860), lib. V, tit. XXXIII, n. 5.

13 Van Espen, *Ius Ecclesiasticum Universum* (5 vols., Lovanii, 1778), Lib. I, Pars II, Sectio I, tit. VI, cap. 7.

his own bishop, to his *proper* priest, or, to another priest who had received delegated jurisdiction from either of the latter.[14]

The strict observance and application of these two canons of the IV Lateran Council implicitly restricted the interritual administration of the sacrament of penance. In those localities where the clergy and laity were all of the same language and rite the interritual administration of this sacrament could be regarded as being of very rare occurrence. Consequently the only places in which its interritual administration could have occurred more or less frequently were the mixed dioceses of the East and West. But in these mixed dioceses the local ordinaries were obliged to provide their subjects of different language and rite with priests who could administer to them according to their language and rite.[15]

Ordinarily the priests thus provided were of the same language and rite as their subjects. If the local ordinaries of such dioceses did not have a sufficient number of qualified priests in their own dioceses to care for the faithful of diverse language and rite, they could make arrangements to acquire the services of such priests from other dioceses.[16] These qualified priests who were given the care of the faithful of different language and rite were their *proper* priests and they alone had ordinary jurisdiction to hear the confessions of their subjects. The faithful could confess to a priest of another language and rite only with the permission of their proper priest or bishop. Therefore it appears that even in these mixed dioceses the

[14] Cf. *supra*, p. 19; *infra*, p. 25.

[15] Cf. *supra*, pp. 17-18.

[16] Friedberg in a footnote to c. 14, X, *de officio iudicis ordinarii,* I, 31, mentions a variant reading of the law as found in the *Compilatio IV* of the *Codex Gracensis 374.* According to this Codex the law read: ". . . pontifices huiusmodi civitatum sive dioecesum *provideant de eadem dioecesi sive de alia viros idoneos* . . ." Friedberg notes in his Prolegomena that the *Codex Gracensis 374,* formerly of the Monastery of St. Lamprecht in Austria, contains all the five *Compilationes* and was drawn up in Italy in the XIV century. He says of it: "Optimus est, quum lectiones Comp. II-IV saepissime cum registro consentiant."—Friedberg, *Corpus Iuris Canonici,* Prolegomena, p. XLIV, n. 4.

interritual administration of the sacrament of penance was of extraordinary occurrence.

Canon IX did not forbid the entrusting of the faithful of some given language and rite to a qualified priest of another language and rite. However, the tendency at that time was certainly not that of entrusting Latins to the care of Oriental bishops or priests.[17] As a matter of fact, the Council of Melfi in the year 1284 explicitly forbade the bishops and abbots of the Kingdom of the Two Sicilies to allow Greeks to celebrate Mass for Latins, or to administer the sacraments to Latins.[18] The policy seemed rather to have been that of entrusting Orientals to the care of Latins.[19] The Greek element in Southern Italy and Sicily dwindled in its numbers from the twelfth to the fifteenth century, so as ultimately to become almost extinct.[20] One of the reasons for the decline in the Greek element was possibly the appointment of Latin priests to parishes in which there was a mixture of Latin and Greek parishioners. If then Latin priests were entrusted with the care of Orientals and were conversant with their language and rite they could in hearing the confessions of their subjects absolve them validly and lawfully.

The possibility at that time of the interritual administration of the sacrament of penance grew out of the case of priests of some given rite, Latin or Oriental, who were entrusted with the care of the faithful who pertained to a rite other than theirs. Such priests who in these extraordinary circumstances heard the confessions of their subjects furnished the sole example of priests who with ordinary jurisdiction administered the sacrament of penance interritually in accordance with the legislation of the IV Lateran Council. The legislation of this Council therefore not merely limited the liberty of the minister and of the recipient of the sacrament of penance in the entire Latin and Maronite Church, but also almost precluded the very possibility of the interritual administration of this sacrament in line with the absolute observance of the laws as enacted in the Council.

[17] Cf. *Fontes,* Series III, Vol. II, p. 319.

[18] Canon IV—Mansi, XXIV, 572.

[19] Cf. *Fontes,* Series III, Vol. II, p. 319.

[20] Petra, *Commentaria ad Constitutiones Apostolicas* (5 vols. in 2, Venetiis, 1729), Commentarium ad Const. XIV, Inn. IV, n. 17.

B. *The Papal Confessional Privileges of Religious*

Not long after the conclusion of the IV Lateran Council the Order of Preachers [21] and of Friars Minor [22] received general papal privileges relative to the administration of the sacrament of penance. These privileges gave to the priests of these Orders who were chosen for the office of preaching the jurisdiction to absolve all the faithful who confessed to them. Moreover the Roman Pontiffs frequently gave Franciscan Friars who were setting out for the Near East special papal privileges to absolve all the faithful dwelling in that territory who had fallen into apostasy, heresy or schism.[23] The grants of these papal privileges did not contain any clause which restricted their use to Latin penitents.

Naturally the wide use of these privileges, especially in the West, caused repercussions among the secular clergy who had the care of souls. The latter felt that the use of these papal confessional privileges involved an infringement of their parochial rights. Pope Boniface VIII (1294-1303) saw fit to regulate and restrict the use of these privileges.[24] This illustrious Pontiff directed religious superiors, in the event that their Orders possessed papal confessional privileges, to choose from their communities priests whom they judged qualified for the hearing of confessions. He further obliged the same religious superiors, either vicariously or personally, to present to the local ordinary for his approval the priests whom they had duly selected. If the local ordinary rejected the first group thus presented by the superior, the latter could present another group.

[21] Gregorius IX, const. *Quoniam,* 10 maii 1227—Potthast, *Regesta Pontificum Romanorum inde ab anno post Christum natum MCXCVIII ad annum MCCCIV* (2 vols., Berolini, 1874-1875), n. 7896 (hereafter cited Potthast).

[22] Gregorius IX, const. *Quoniam,* 6 apr. 1237—*Bullarium Franciscanum Romanorum Pontificum Constitutiones, Epistolas ac Diplomata Continens* (9 vols., Vols. I-III, ed. Joannis H. Sbaraleae, Romae, 1759-1765), I, 24 (hereafter cited *Bull. Franc.*).

[23] Gregorius IX, const. *Pro zelo,* 17 maii 1233—*Bull. Franc.*, I, 103; const. *Pro zelo,* 30 ian. 1238—*Bull. Franc.*, I, 231; Potthast, n. 10513; Innocentius IV, const. *Pro zelo,* 4 oct. 1244—*Bull. Franc.*, I, 351; Potthast, n. 11462; const. *Pro zelo,* 15 iul. 1250—*Bull. Franc.*, I, 546; Potthast, n. 14014.

[24] Const. *Super cathedram,* 18 febr. 1300—c. 2, *de sepulturis,* III 7, in Clem.; Potthast, n. 24913.

If episcopal approval was denied also to this second group, then the latter presentees automatically received papal approval to use their papal privileges. They could validly and lawfully absolve anyone in the diocese who confessed to them.[25]

Except for minor variations this became the normal mode of procedure relative to the use of the papal confessional privileges which religious Orders possessed, and it continued in use until the time of the Council of Trent.[26] The common participation of all religious Orders in whatever papal privileges had been granted to any one specific religious Order was a juridical fact which was recognized at that time. This juridical fact implied that any papal confessional privilege which had originally been granted to one Order came to be shared in common by all religious Orders alike. Consequently Pope Leo X (1513-1521) in 1519 was able to state that the Dominicans, Franciscans, Augustinians, Carmelites, Servites and Minims held all their confessional privileges in common.[27]

In spite of the existence of the papal confessional privileges the annual confession prescribed by the IV Lateran Council had to be made to one's proper priest or to some other priest with the proper priest's permission.[28] After the year 1516 even this provision seemed to have lost its binding force, for Pope Leo X (1513-1521) declared that the faithful who had confessed their sins to priests religious who had been approved by the ordinary, or even to those who had been unjustly refused approval, fulfilled by means of such a confession the law regarding the annual confession as imposed by the IV Lateran Council.[29]

Since there was no clause which restricted the use of these papal confessional privileges in consequence of a divergence of rite between

[25] *Loc. cit.*

[26] Cf. Leo X, const. *Dum intra,* 19 dec. 1516, § 6—*Fontes,* n. 72.

[27] Const. *Dudum per nos,* 10 dec. 1519—*Bullarum Diplomatum et Privilegiorum Sanctorum Romanorum Pontificum Taurinensis Editio* (24 vols. et Appendix, Augustae Taurinorum, 1857-1872), V, 733 (hereafter cited *Bull. Rom.*).

[28] Alexander IV, const. *Cum olim,* 18 ian. 1259—Potthast, n. 17452; Martinus IV, const. *Ad fructus uberes,* 13 dec. 1281—Potthast, n. 21821; Sixtus IV, const. *Vices illius,* anno 1475—c. 2, *de treuga et pace,* I 9, in Extravag. com.

[29] Const. *Dum intra,* 19 dec. 1516, § 6—*Bull. Rom.,* V, 685-689.

confessor and penitent, it is quite probable that the interritual administration of the sacrament of penance was not uncommon in Southern Italy and Sicily, where there were Catholics who followed Byzantine ritual and customs.[30] Its interritual administration was probably even more common in the vast mission fields of the East. Many religious Orders founded abbeys and monasteries in the Latin Empire of Constantinople.[31]

The Order of Friars Minor from its infancy was especially interested in the Oriental Christians. Before 1222 Franciscan provinces had been established in Antioch and in Constantinople.[32] In 1268 the Province of Antioch became the Province of Syria or of the Holy Land with houses in Cyprus, Syria and Palestine under its jurisdiction.[33] Pope Clement V (1305-1314) granted special faculties to Franciscan missionaries who were setting out to work among the people of practically every nationality in the East.[34] Before 1384 the Franciscans had erected the Vicariate of Bosnia, which had 35 houses in the Balkans; the Vicariate of Russia, which counted 15 houses, the majority of them having been established among the Ruthenians; the Vicariate of Lithuania, which had 5 houses under its jurisdiction.[35]

Other Latin religious Orders were also engaged in missionary activity in the East. To give a detailed account of their labors during this period would be to exceed the purpose of this work. The point is that Latin missionaries were working in the East among Oriental Christians. It is certain, too, that they were instrumental in reuniting thousands of Oriental schismatics and heretics to the Church of Rome.[36] To effect the perfect reunion of individual souls

[30] *Statistica con cenni storici della Gerarchia e dei Fedeli di Rito Orientale* (Sacra Congregazione Orientale, Roma: Tipografia Poliglotta Vaticana, 1932), pp. 116-117 (hereafter cited *Statistica*).

[31] *Fontes,* Series III, Vol. II, p. 126.

[32] Huber, *A Documented History of the Franciscan Order* (1182-1517) (Milwaukee, Wis. and Washington, D. C.: The Nowiny Publishing Apostolate, Inc., 1944), p. 706 (hereafter cited Huber).

[33] *Ibidem,* p. 755.

[34] Wadding, *Annales Minorum* (3. ed., 27 vols., Quaracchi, 1931-1934), VI, 97.

[35] Huber, p. 708.

[36] Huber, pp. 763-764.

with God and with His Church the administration of the sacrament of penance was necessary. Therefore the Latin missionaries had to absolve Oriental schismatics and heretics to perfect their work. It cannot be assumed that all the missionaries who were laboring in the East were of the same rite as that of the Oriental Christians among whom they labored. The majority of the missionaries were Latins. Consequently the interritual administration of the sacrament of penance must not have been such an extraordinary occurrence for these Latin missionaries.

Although the legislation of the IV General Council of the Lateran practically eliminated the possibility of the interritual administration of the sacrament of penance as far as the parochial and secular clergy of the period were concerned, the papal confessional privileges which were granted to religious Orders did not imply the same restrictive effect. As a matter of fact religious, especially missionaries, who used their papal privileges to absolve penitents of a rite other than their own, evinced the ordinary example of the interritual administration of the sacrament of penance during this period.

C. *Legislation from the Council of Trent to the Code*

The Council of Trent explicitly taught that no priest could pronounce valid sacramental absolution unless he had ordinary or delegated jurisdiction over the penitent.[37] It likewise decreed that no priest could hear the confessions of seculars, even of priests, unless he held a parochial benefice or was judged competent by the bishop and had obtained episcopal approval.[38] This Tridentine legislation took away the power, formerly possessed by priests who had the care of souls, of delegating confessional jurisdiction over their subjects.[39] Priests who held parochial benefices, however, could absolve their parishioners even outside the diocese without the approval of the bishop of that diocese.[40] Within the territorial limits of their pa-

[37] Sess. XIV, *de poenitentia,* c. 7.

[38] Sess. XXIII, *de ref.,* c. 15.

[39] Cf. *supra,* pp. 18-19.

[40] S. C. C., *Posnanien.,* 19 nov., 3 dec. 1707, ad 1—*Fontes,* n. 3058.

rochial benefice they could also hear the confessions of non-parishioners.[41]

Tridentine law did not make any mention of the diversity of rite which might exist between confessor and penitent, nor did it limit the use of confessional jurisdiction on the basis of the existence of such a diversity. Consequently, after the Council of Trent priests who held parochial benefices could absolve their parishioners anywhere; priests delegated for the whole diocese, or also religious who had episcopal approval to use their papal confessional privileges, could hear within the diocese the confessions of all the faithful who came to them. The jurisdiction of these confessors was not limited because of their rite or that of their penitents.

Not long after the reunion of the Ukranian Ruthenians, which began in 1595,[42] difficulties relative to the interritual administration of the sacrament of penance arose between these Oriental Catholics and their Latin neighbors. Apparently both the Latin and the Ruthenian bishops forbade their subjects to confess their sins to priests of the other rite. The Holy See upbraided the Latin and the Ruthenian bishops for thus restricting their subjects' liberty.[43] The bishops of both rites were told that they must not prohibit their subjects from confessing their sins to priests of the other rite who were approved by their local ordinary.[44]

The Holy See on various occasions thereafter gave its approval to the interritual administration of the sacrament of penance. In 1647 the Sacred Congregation for the Propagation of the Faith declared that Oriental patriarchs and bishops could not prevent Latin missionaries from administering the sacrament of penance to penitents of the Oriental rites.[45] In 1715 the Holy Office told Latin and Oriental bishops that they were free to approve priests of any rite

[41] S. C. C., *Vilnen.*, 25 iun. 1639, ad 5—*Fontes*, n. 2607; *Burgi S. Sepulchri*, 20 sept. 1698, ad 4—*Fontes*, n. 2966.

[42] Clemens VIII, const. *Magnus Dominus*, 23 dec. 1595—*Fonti*, Serie I, Fasc. VIII, *Studi storici sulle fonti di diritto canonico orientale* (Roma: Tipografia Poliglotta Vaticana, 1932), 601 (hereafter cited *Fonti*, Serie I, Fasc. VIII).

[43] S. C. de Prop. Fide, decr. 5 iun. 1626—*Fontes*, n. 4757.

[44] S. C. de Prop. Fide, *loc. cit.*

[45] (C. G.), 26 apr. 1647—*Coll. S. C. P. F.*, n. 116.

as confessors for all the faithful in their dioceses.[46] In 1838 the Sacred Congregation for the Propagation of the Faith again insisted that Oriental bishops could not by means of any general prohibition forbid their subjects to make a sacramental confession to Latin missionaries.[47]

It seems that during the period from the Council of Trent until the promulgation of the Latin Code the Holy See on only one occasion prohibited the interritual administration of the sacrament of penance. Italo-Greek priests were forbidden to hear the confessions of Latins except in a case of necessity.[48] However, this prohibition was not absolute, for the Holy See permitted Latin ordinaries, according to their prudence and discretion, to approve competent Italo-Greek priests for hearing the confessions of the faithful of both the Latin and the Greek rites.[49] The reason for this particular prohibition evidently did not derive from the divergent rite of the minister or of the recipient of the sacrament of penance, for the Sacred Congregation for the Propagation of the Faith on several occasions thereafter was able to state that "the Holy See has never been accustomed to limit in any way the Christian's freedom in such a delicate matter as is the sacrament of penance. She has always wished that anyone be permitted to confess his sins to any approved confessor according to his preference. She has never prohibited any approved confessor from hearing in his own church the confession of any Catholic whatsoever who presented himself in the sacred tribunal . . . There has never been on this point any distinction of rite, since the administration of this sacrament does not effect any change of rite." [50]

[46] 5 dec. 1715—*Coll. Lac.*, II, 506b.

[47] (C. G.), 11 dec. 1838, ad 12, 13—*Fontes,* n. 4778.

[48] Clemens VIII, decr. *Presbyteri Graeci,* 31 aug. 1595, § 3—*Bull. Rom.*, X, 212; Benedictus XIV, const. *Etsi pastoralis,* 26 maii 1742, § V, n. 5—*Fontes,* n. 328.

[49] Benedictus XIV, *ibidem,* n. 6—*Fontes,* n. 328.

[50] Instr. (ad Archiep. Aleppen.), 2 iun. 1835: "La S. Sede ha ritenuto sempre la massima, che non si deve vincolare in alcun modo la libertà de' cristiani in un punto così delicato, quale è la sacramentale Confessione, ed ha voluto sempre che fosse lecito a ciascuno di manifestare le sue colpe a quello tra i sacri ministri approvati, che gli fosse più a grado. Non ha egualmente mai proibito ad un confessore approvato di ascoltare nella propria Chiesa la

Article 2. The Law of the Latin Code

The Latin Code evinces the first general legislation of the Church which gives explicit approval to the interritual administration of the sacrament of penance.[51] Since the Church gives both the confessor and the penitent definite rights relative to the interritual administration of the sacrament of penance, the interritual right of each will be taken up for separate consideration.

A. *The Interritual Right of the Confessor*

Canon 872 reiterates the teaching of the Church which requires that the minister of the sacrament of penance be a validly ordained priest who possesses ordinary or delegated jurisdiction over the penitent. The canons and canonists of the Oriental as well as of the Latin Church had given expression to these same requirements in the minister of this sacrament long before the promulgation of the Latin Code. The eminent canonist of the Oriental Church, Theodore Balsamon (ca. 1140-ca. 1195), declared that in the Church of the East only priests who had the permission of the bishop could hear confessions.[52] The collections of Gratian and of Bernard of Pavia [53] as also later official ecclesiastical sources [54] give ample evidence of the common canonical doctrine of the Church in the West.

In an effort to refute the widespread erroneous teaching of the Protestant Reformation, the Council of Trent found it necessary to

confessioni di qualunque siasi cattolico, che si presentasse al sacro tribunale . . . Non si è fatta poi mai alcuna distinzione di rito, giacchè l'amministrazione di tal sagramento non porta seco alcun cambiamento di rito . . ."—*Fontes*, n. 4757. Cf. also instr. (ad Deleg. Ap. Aegypti), 30 apr. 1862, n. 2—*Fontes*, n. 4857.

[51] Cf. Coronata, *Tractatus Canonicus de Sacramentis* (3 vols., Taurini-Romae: Marietti, 1943-1946), I, n. 460 (hereafter cited *De Sacramentis*).

[52] "Alibi diximus, solis tributum esse sacerdotibus confessionum ratiocinia cum episcopali permissu."—*Fonti*, Serie II, Fasc. V, *Textus Selecti ex Operibus Commentatorum Byzantinorum Iuris Ecclesiastici* (Romae: Typis Polyglottis Vaticanis, 1939), n. 404 (hereafter cited *Fonti*, Serie II, Fasc. V); cf. also Thomassinus, Pars I, lib. II, cap. 12, n. 9.

[53] Cf. *supra*, p. 19, footnote 12.

[54] Cf. *supra*, pp. 18-19, 25-26.

define in express terms what had been the common doctrine concerning the nature of sacramental absolution and the necessity of confessional jurisdiction.[55] This Council solemnly taught that sacramental absolution partakes of the nature of a judicial act. Since the confessor acts as a judge within the sacred tribunal of penance, he must have the authority necessary to pronounce sentence.[56] To pronounce valid sacramental absolution, therefore, every confessor must possess judicial jurisdiction in the internal sacramental forum.[57]

Any exercise of judicial jurisdiction necessarily presupposes the subjection of the person judged to the power of the judge. The valid exercise of jurisdiction in the internal sacramental forum likewise requires that the same relation of subject to superior exist between the penitent and the confessor.[58] The Code states it as a principle that jurisdiction can be directly exercised over subjects only.[59]

Now, one becomes a subject of jurisdiction in the Church in different ways. A person becomes a subject of the Church through valid baptism; [60] of a particular parish or diocese, by reason of residence therein; [61] of a particular rite, ordinarily through valid baptism in that rite; [62] of a religious institute, by religious profession.[63] Thus it is that parishioners by reason of domicile or quasi-domicile are subject to the sacramental jurisdiction of their pastors; members of an ordinariate are likewise subject to the jurisdiction of their ordinary.[64] There exists as it were a personal relationship between these subjects and their superiors' jurisdiction in the internal sac-

[55] Sess. XIV, *de poenitentia,* c. 7, can. 9; sess. XXIII, *de ref.,* c. 15.

[56] Sess. XIV, *de poenitentia,* c. 7; cf. also St. Thomas, *Summa Theologica,* suppl., q. 17, a. 2; Willis, "Ius Clavium iuxta Sanctum Thomam"—*The Jurist* (Washington, D. C., 1941—), I (1941), 108-124.

[57] Cf. *supra,* pp. 2-3.

[58] St. Thomas, *Summa Theologica,* suppl., q. 20, a. 3; Billot, *De Ecclesiae Sacramentis* (7. ed., 2 vols., Romae: Apud Aedes Universitatis Gregorianae, 1929-1931), I, 19-20 (hereafter cited *De Sacramentis*).

[59] Canon 201, § 1.

[60] Canon 87.

[61] Canon 94.

[62] Canon 98, § 1.

[63] Canon 578.

[64] Cf. canons 92, 94, § 1, and 873, § 1.

ramental forum.[65] Consequently such superiors can pronounce valid sacramental absolution in favor of penitents who are subject to their personal jurisdiction.[66]

Jurisdiction may also be exercised over those who, although they are not personally subject to the superior's jurisdictional power, become subject to it according to definite prescriptions of law.[67] For this reason travelers (*peregrini*) are subject to certain particular territorial laws; [68] those guilty of ecclesiastical crimes become subject to the territorial jurisdiction of the judge of the place where the crime was committed.[69] In the same way confessors with ordinary or delegated *local* jurisdiction may pronounce valid sacramental absolution even in favor of travelers (*peregrini*).[70]

Like all confessors, the interritual confessor must possess personal or local jurisdiction over the penitent if he is to pronounce valid sacramental absolution. The Latin Code explicitly approves of the interritual administration of the sacrament of penance when the confessor possesses local jurisdiction.[71]. Elsewhere it gives implicit approval to this practice.

Thus all confessors who have ordinary jurisdiction [72] may absolve their subjects anywhere.[73] All validly ordained priests can absolve any baptized person in danger of death.[74] Superiors of exempt clerical religious institutes or their delegates may hear the confessions of the subjects juridically confided to their care.[75] Confessors of men religious [76] and of women religious [77] may absolve all those for whom they are competent according to the prescriptions of law. All confessors who possess maritime faculties according to

65 Cf. *infra,* pp. 52-53.

66 Cf. *infra,* Chapter IV.

67 Coronata, *Institutiones,* I, n. 282; Beste, *Introductio,* p. 218.

68 Canon 14, § 1, 2°.

69 Canon 1566.

70 Canon 881, § 1; cf. also Beste, *loc. cit.*

71 Canon 881, § 1.

72 Cf. Canon 873.

73 Canon 881, § 2.

74 Canon 882.

75 Canons 873, § 2, and 875, § 1.

76 Canons 518-519 and 528.

77 Canons 520-524.

canon 883 can use their jurisdiction, in keeping with the limitations of the law, in favor of all in whose case the requirements set by the law have been fulfilled. The confessors of cardinals [78] and of bishops [79] are competent to absolve all those who are subject to their personal jurisdiction.

In all these cases the Code does not advert to any diversity of rite between confessor and penitent. But in all these cases there is the possibility that such a diversity may in reality exist. Although the confessors' jurisdiction may be limited for other reasons,[80] it is in no way restricted by the Code on the score of diversity of rite.

B. *The Interritual Right of the Penitent*

In matters of the external judicial forum the plaintiff or the defendant does not have extensive liberty in the choice of a competent forum.[81] In matters of the internal forum the Church is much more liberal, for canon 905 states that the faithful have the right to confess their sins to the duly authorized confessor of their choice, even though he belong to a rite other than theirs.[82] This canon allows the penitent almost unrestricted liberty in the choice of a confessor. Ever desirous of removing any unnecessary odium or repugnance which might be connected with sacramental confession, the Church in its present discipline permits a penitent to confess his sins to any confessor of his choice. The only condition is that the confessor selected by him be otherwise competent according to the prescriptions of law.

The faithful can always confess their sins to any confessor who has personal jurisdiction over them in the internal sacramental forum, such as their pastor, their ordinary or the delegates of the latter.[83] They may also in virtue of canon 881, § 1, confess their sins to any priest with local jurisdiction in any place within the limits of his local competence. Even travelers (*peregrini*) or Catholics of a di-

[78] Canon 239, § 1, 2°.

[79] Canon 349, § 1, 1°.

[80] E.g., canon 878, § 1.

[81] Cf. canons 1556-1568.

[82] "Cuivis fideli integrum est confessario legitime approbato etiam alius ritus, cui maluerit, peccata sua confiteri."

[83] Cf. *supra*, pp. 29-30.

verse rite who are not otherwise personally subject to the jurisdiction of a confessor are free to subject themselves to any local tribunal of their choice. The Church as it were thus extends the judicial axiom of the external forum, *actor sequitur forum rei*, to the internal sacramental forum. The penitent who is simultaneously the plaintiff and the defendant within the sacred tribunal is given the choice of any local forum as long as the judge therein is otherwise competent.[84]

While canon 905 gives the faithful wide liberty in the choice of a confessor, it at the same time expresses the Church's general approval of the interritual administration of the sacrament of penance. Provided the confessor who is selected is otherwise competent, the penitent has the right to the interritual administration of this sacrament. Assuredly the Church in its present written law gives the faithful interritual freedom in the matter of sacramental confession.

It is certain that all the faithful of the Latin rite participate in the benefits of this legislation. Do not the faithful of the Oriental rites enjoy the same freedom? According to canon 1 the law of the Latin Code does not pertain to Orientals unless they are expressly mentioned or are included *ex ipsa rei natura*. Canon 905 which grants to the faithful freedom to confess their sins to the approved confessor of their choice certainly has as its immediate purpose the good of souls which is thereby accomplished.[85] The Holy See has declared on different occasions that in such a delicate matter as is sacramental confession there should be no discrimination between the faithful merely on the score of diversity of rite.[86] It seems therefore that the faithful of the Oriental rites also participate in the benefits legislated in canon 905.

It also must be remembered that the previous decrees and decisions of the Holy See which form the basic sources for this law of

[84] Augustine, *A Commentary on the New Code of Canon Law* (8 vols., St. Louis, 1918-1922), IV, 285 (hereafter cited *Commentary*).

[85] Cappello, *Tractatus Canonico-Moralis de Sacramentis*, Vol. II, *De Poenitentia* (3. ed., Taurinorum Augustae: Marietti, 1939), nn. 406, 1038-1039 (hereafter cited *De Poenitentia*); Duskie, *The Canonical Status of Orientals in the United States*, pp. 127-128.

[86] Cf. S. C. de Prop. Fide, instr. (ad Archiep. Aleppen.), 2 iun. 1835—*Fontes*, n. 4757; *supra*, pp. 26-28.

the Latin Code granted the same freedom to penitents of the Oriental rites as to those of the Latin rite.[87] The particular laws of various Oriental rites expressly grant the same interritual freedom to the penitent.[88] The particular law of the Ruthenians in the United States and in Canada states that the faithful of the Greek-Ruthenian rite can confess their sins to a priest of the Latin rite who is approved by his own bishop.[89] Authors on the subject commonly agree that the faithful of the Oriental rites enjoy the same freedom of choice as do the faithful of the Latin rite.[90]

This official and universal written approval of the interritual administration of the sacrament of penance exists as a governing factor relative to the legislative competence of all inferior legislators. No one, except the Bishop of Rome, could enact legislation contrary to the interritual right of penitents or confessors. Neither an ordinary nor a pastor could forbid his subjects in general to confess their sins to confessors of another rite who are otherwise competent. Neither could any ordinary lawfully prevent confessors, otherwise competent, from absolving penitents who belonged to a diverse rite. Such prohibitions, if invoked simply on the score of diversity of rite, would be unlawful restrictions of an interritual

[87] S. C. de Prop. Fide, instr. (ad Archiep. Aleppen.), 2 iun. 1835—*Fontes,* n. 4757; (C. G.), 11 dec. 1838, ad 12, 13—*Fontes,* n. 4778; instr. (ad Deleg. Ap. Aegypti), 30 apr. 1862, n. 2°—*Fontes,* n. 4857.

[88] E.g., Synodus Montis Libani (1736), pars II, cap. IV, n. 8—Mansi, XXXVIII, 53-54; Ius Particulare Ruthenorum—*Fonti,* Serie I, Fasc. XI, *Disciplina Bizantina, (Rutheni): Ius Particulare Ruthenorum* (Roma: Tipografia Poliglotta Vaticana, 1933), nn. 494-495; 497-498 (hereafter cited *Fonti* Serie I, Fasc. XI).

[89] S. C. Or., decr. *Cum data fuerit,* 1 mart. 1929, art. 31—*AAS,* XXI (1929), 15; Bouscaren, *Digest,* I, 14; *Graeci-Rutheni Ritus,* 24 maii 1930, art. 36—*AAS,* XXII (1930), 35; Bouscaren, *op. cit.,* I, 36.

[90] Cappello, *loc. cit.*; Augustine, *Commentary,* IV, 347; Blat, *Commentarium Textus Codicis Iuris Canonici* (5 vols. in 6, Romae, 1919-1927), Lib. III, Pars I, *De Sacramentis,* 279 (hereafter cited *De Sacramentis*); Coronata, *De Sacramentis,* I, n. 460; Duskie, *loc. cit.*; Diederichs, *The Jurisdiction of the Latin Ordinaries Over Their Oriental Subjects,* p. 96; Dausend, *Das interrituelle Recht im Codex Iuris Canonici* (Paderborn: Schöningh, 1939), p. 130 (hereafter cited *Das interrituelle Recht*); Petrani, *De Relatione Iuridica inter Diversos Ritus in Ecclesia Catholica* (Taurini et Romae: Marietti, 1930), p. 87 (hereafter cited *De Relatione Iuridica inter Diversos Ritus*).

right given to the faithful by the highest legislative authority in the Church.[91]

Since the Church gives the faithful the right of confessing their sins to any *competent* confessor of any rite, confessors would also act unlawfully were they to refuse to hear the confessions of any of the faithful for the reason simply that the latter belongs to a different rite. Such a refusal would be contrary to the common law of the Church as expressed in canon 905.

[91] Cappello, *De Poenitentia,* n. 406; Duskie, *op. cit.,* p. 128; Augustine, *loc. cit.*

CHAPTER III

THE INTERRITUAL CONFESSOR WITH LOCAL JURISDICTION

JUST as no civilian can sit in judgment in civil courts unless public authority has assigned him subjects over whom he may exercise his superior power, so in the Church of Christ no priest can pass judgment in the internal sacramental forum unless public ecclesiastical authority has granted him such superior sacred power either in consequence of his assignment to an office to which that power is attached, or through the committing of such power to him personally.[1] Just as a civil judge who exceeds the personal, territorial or material limits of his competence acts invalidly, so too the ecclesiastical judge in the internal sacramental forum who exceeds the personal, territorial or material limits of his jurisdictional power acts invalidly whenever the act of exceeding is forbidden under pain of nullity.[2] The knowledge of the limits of his competence is of the utmost importance to every judge. For the judge who pronounces sentence in the sacred tribunal of penance such knowledge is even more important than for him who occupies the bench in civil courts.

The interritual confessor with local jurisdiction must know the territorial limits of the sacramental power which he possesses. He must also know what penitents he is competent to bind and loose. The purpose of this chapter is to determine the territorial and personal extent of the interritual confessor's local jurisdiction.

ARTICLE 1. THE LAW OF THE LATIN CODE

Canon 881, § 1, states that all priests, secular or religious, if they are approved for hearing confessions in a given place and if they possess ordinary or delegated jurisdiction, can validly and lawfully absolve within their local competence all penitents who approach them, irrespective of the elements of domicile or rite involved in the

[1] Canons 872 and 197, § 1.

[2] Cf., e.g., canons 876; 874, § 1; 884; 893; 895.

case.[3] The very purpose of this law seems to consist in the constitution of an indubitable legal norm whereby confessors who possess local jurisdiction can measure the personal field of their local competence.[4] Besides furnishing a legal norm for the solution of potentially disturbing problems, this canon at the same time gives an explicit approval for all confessors of the Latin rite, if they possess local jurisdiction, to administer the sacrament of penance to penitents of the Oriental rites.

Do not confessors of the Oriental rites who possess local jurisdiction likewise enjoy the benefits of this law of the Church? That this law applies equally to local confessors of the Oriental rites follows from the penitential liberty granted to the faithful by the supreme legislative authority in the Church. For the same reasons as stated above,[5] it seems that irrespective of their rite all confessors who possess local jurisdiction enjoy the same personal competence within the field of their local jurisdiction.[6]

Although it is true that according to their particular law Italo-Greek confessors could absolve Latins only in danger of death,[7] this fact does not militate against the present law of the Code. The jurisdiction which the Italo-Greek confessors possessed must be considered to have been personal rather than local. Furthermore, the law itself permitted the local Latin ordinary to extend their jurisdiction so that suitable Italo-Greek confessors could also absolve penitents of the Latin rite.[8]

There is no doubt that in the United States and in Canada local confessors of the Oriental rites have the right to absolve all penitents

[3] "Omnes utriusque cleri sacerdotes ad audiendas confessiones approbati in aliquo loco, sive ordinaria sive delegata iurisdictione instructi, possunt etiam vagos ac peregrinos ex alia dioecesi vel paroecia ad sese accedentes, itemque catholicos cuiusque ritus orientalis, valide et licite absolvere."

[4] Blat, *De Sacramentis*, p. 229.

[5] Cf. *supra*, pp. 32-33.

[6] Cf. Cappello, *De Poenitentia*, nn. 406; 1038-1039; Duskie, *The Canonical Status of Orientals in the United States*, pp. 125-127; Dausend *Das interrituelle Recht*, pp. 130-136; Petrani, *De Relatione Iuridica inter Diversos Ritus*, pp. 87-89; Diederichs, *The Jurisdiction of Latin Ordinaries over Their Oriental Subjects*, p. 96.

[7] Cf. *supra*, p. 27.

[8] Cf. *supra*, ibid.

who approach their local sacramental tribunal irrespective of their domicile or rite. Local confessors of the Ruthenian rite are explicitly given the right to absolve Latins.[9] Since all other priests of the Oriental rites who have the care of souls in North America are subject to the local ordinary of the Latin rite in all matters of discipline, they must receive from him their local jurisdiction either by way of delegation or through their assignment to an office to which local jurisdiction is automatically attached.[10]

Unless the contrary is expressed, their local jurisdiction will have the same extent and limitations as the ordinary or delegated jurisdiction similarly granted to priests of the Latin rite in accordance with the law in force in the particular locality.[11] Although the local ordinaries may limit delegated local jurisdiction for other reasons,[12] it seems that they would act unlawfully if in granting a priest of an Oriental rite *local* jurisdiction they at the same time limited the use of that jurisdiction to penitents of a particular rite.[13]

Canon 881, § 1, also raises another question which was the subject of dispute among authors in the past. By what right do local confessors exercise jurisdiction over travelers (*peregrini*)? In virtue of canon 881, § 1, there is no dispute now as to whether or not local confessors *can* absolve travelers. However, there are still divergent opinions regarding the nature of the jurisdictional power whereby local confessors absolve travelers of the Latin rite as well as of the Oriental rites.

St. Alphonsus (1696-1787) in discussing the problem stated that local confessors could absolve travelers because of the universal custom and the tacit consent of the ordinary of the travelers.[14] In another part of his moral treatise, when discussing absolution from reserved sins, he maintained that local confessors could absolve

[9] Cf. *supra*, p. 33.

[10] Cf. S. C. Or., decr. *Qua sollerti*, 23 dec. 1929, nn. 10-17—*AAS*, XXII (1930), 99-105; Bouscaren, *Digest*, I, 22-23; also Diederichs, *op. cit.*, pp. 95-96; Duskie, *op. cit.*, p. 127.

[11] Cf. *infra*, pp. 47-48.

[12] Canon 878.

[13] Cf. *supra*, pp. 30-34.

[14] *Theologia Moralis* (ed. L. Gaudé, 4 vols. Romae, 1905-1912), lib. VI, n. 569.

travelers (*peregrini*) in virtue of the will of the Church, which by its approval of the existing custom granted the requisite jurisdiction.[15] Ballerini (1805-1881)-Palmieri (1829-1909) denied that jurisdiction could be obtained in consequence of any established custom. The existing custom was merely the expression of the tacit consent of the proper ordinary of the travelers, in virtue of which any local confessor could absolve such penitents.[16]

In our own day Cappello and others maintain that the power whereby pastors within their parochial boundaries can absolve non-parishioners is delegated to them by the common law in consequence of the ruling contained in canon 881, § 1.[17] Coronata does not seem to be consistent. In one place he states that the power of a pastor to absolve travelers within his local competence seems to be part and parcel of his ordinary confessional jurisdiction.[18] But in commenting on canon 881, § 1, he holds that jurisdiction over travelers is delegated through this canon to all confessors who have local jurisdiction where the confessions are heard.[19] Other authors hold that local confessors can absolve travelers in virtue either of their ordinary local jurisdiction or of the delegated local jurisdiction which they have received from the local ordinary.[20]

The opinion of those who hold that the local confessor's jurisdiction over travelers is delegated by the common law does not seem to be in keeping with the present legislation of the Church. Th purpose of canon 881, § 1, was to express precisely and clearly the personal extent of the local confessor's ordinary or delegated jurisdiction. Its purpose was not that of giving added jurisdiction to that which was already possessed, but rather that of furnishing

[15] *Ibidem,* n. 588.

[16] *Opus Theologicum Morale* (7 vols., Prati, 1889-1893), V, n. 379.

[17] Cappello, *De Poenitentia,* n. 384, 4; cf. also Kelly, *The Jurisdiction of the Confessor* (New York, Cincinnati, Chicago: Benziger Brothers, 1929), pp. 44-45.

[18] *De Sacramentis,* I, n. 349b.

[19] *De Sacramentis,* I, n. 358.

[20] Aertnys-Damen, *Theologia Moralis secundum doctrinam S. Alfonsi* (15. ed., 2 vols., Romae: Marietti, 1947), II, nn. 343, 348 and 383 (hereafter cited *Theologia Moralis*); Augustine, *Commentary,* IV, 285; Blat, *De Sacramentis,* p. 230; Vermeersch-Creusen, *Epitome,* II, n. 151.

added liberty to confessors and penitents. Canon 197, § 1, states that any jurisdiction which is attached by law to an office is ordinary. Consequently any power which is attached by law to be enjoyed by the incumbent of an ecclesiastical office must be considered as ordinary, and not as delegated by the common law.[21]

Local ordinaries, pastors and others holding an office which is equivalent in law to that of a pastor have ecclesiastical offices. They have ordinary *personal* jurisdiction over the members of their ordinariate or of their parish or quasi-parish respectively, so that they can anywhere exercise their jurisdiction of the internal sacramental forum over those who are personally subject to them.[22] They also have ordinary *local* jurisdiction of the sacramental forum within their respective territories.[23]

The local extent of the sacramental jurisdiction of the local ordinary is the whole ordinariate; that of the local pastor is the parochial territory.[24] As a result they can exercise their ordinary *local* jurisdiction over all penitents, even travelers (*peregrini*), who approach their local tribunal. All other confessors who desire delegated local jurisdiction must receive it from the ordinary of the place where the confessions are to be heard.[25] This delegated local jurisdiction which may be exercised also over travelers (*peregrini*) derives not from the common law but from the local ordinary. By the very fact that travelers confess their sins to a confessor who has ordinary or delegated local jurisdiction they become subject to the local jurisdiction which he possesses.[26] Consequently, the opinion which holds

21 "Ordinariam dicemus omnem potestatem iure concessam ei qui verum officium obtinet, v.g. Ordinariis, parochis, etc., nisi contrarium ex ipso textu appareat. . ."—Vermeersch-Creusen, *op. cit.*, I, n. 314, 3.

22 Canon 881, § 2.

23 Canon 873, § 1.

24 Canon 873, § 1.

25 Canon 874, § 1.

26 St. Alphonsus indicated this when he said: "Peregrini, stante hodierna consuetudine . . . nempe quod absolvuntur ubique a quocumque confessario approbato, hodie non amplius absolvuntur ex voluntate eorum Episcoporum, sed ex voluntate Ecclesiae, quae talem consuetudinem approbando, *tribuit facultatem ut habeantur tamquam incolae loci ubi confitentur.*"—*Theologia Moralis,* lib. VI, n. 588. Cf. also Cappello, *De Poenitentia,* n. 379; Blat, *De Sacramentis,* p. 230; Vermeersch-Creusen, *Epitome,* II, n. 145.

that local confessors absolve travelers in virtue of their ordinary local jurisdiction or of the delegated local jurisdiction which they have received from the local ordinary seems to stand as the more acceptable doctrine.

The text of canon 881, § 1, is clear enough except for the meaning of the word *approbati*. The exact significance of this word is not evident at first glance. Some authors simply state that the word means *possessed of jurisdiction*.[27] The word must have at least this meaning.[28] The context seems to indicate however that *approbati* has a more comprehensive connotation. According to the law all priests, secular and religious, when *approved* for hearing confessions in a given place, may *validly and lawfully* absolve therein all penitents who approach their local tribunal. Canon 874, § 1, states that religious who have received faculties from the local ordinary cannot *lawfully* use their delegated jurisdiction without at least the presumed permission of their religious superior. Confessors who desire to exercise their local jurisdiction in a church to which they are not attached are also required to have at least the presumed permission of the rector.[29]

The word *approbati* as used in this particular law therefore means more than simply *possessed of jurisdiction*. It means that local confessors must possess local jurisdiction and at the same time have permission to exercise their jurisdiction when such permission is required by law.[30]. Local jurisdiction is required for validity; permission is sometimes required for the lawful use of the jurisdiction which the local confessor possesses. Consequently the interritual confessor must also comply with these requisites if he would exercise his local jurisdictional power not only validly but also lawfully.

The existence of two distinct ritual jurisdictions in the United

[27] Cappello, *De Poenitentia*, n. 376, 4; Kelly, *The Jurisdiction of the Confessor*, p. 41; Motry, *Diocesan Faculties According to the Code of Canon Law*, The Catholic University of America Canon Law Studies, n. 16 (Washington, D. C.: The Catholic University of America, 1922), p. 96.

[28] Cf. canon 872.

[29] Canon 484, § 1; Kelly, *op. cit.*, p. 48; Sabetti-Barrett, *Compendium Theologiae Moralis* (30. ed., New York: Pustet, 1924), p. 739 (hereafter cited *Compendium*).

[30] Coronata, *De Sacramentis*, I, n. 358; Augustine, *Commentary*, IV, 283.

States and Canada necessarily affects the local competence of confessors who possess local jurisdiction. The local jurisdiction for the sacramental forum which proceeds from the local Latin ordinaries does not extend to those churches or oratories which are under the exclusive jurisdiction of the Ruthenian ordinaries. Similarly, although the personal-territorial jurisdiction of the Ruthenian ordinaries extends over the entire territory of the United States or over large portions of Canada, the churches and oratories which are under the exclusive jurisdiction of the local Latin ordinaries do not fall within the scope of their jurisdiction. Therefore, although the churches or oratories which are under the exclusive jurisdiction of an ordinary of the Latin or of the Ruthenian rite are physically situated within the territorial boundaries of both ordinariates, they are from a juridic standpoint outside the local competence of either the one or the other ordinary.[31]

From this general principle it follows that confessors who have received *local* jurisdiction from the Latin ordinaries would exceed the limits of their *local* competence were they to hear confessions in Ruthenian churches or oratories in the United States or Canada. Similarly confessors who have received *local* jurisdiction from the Ruthenian ordinaries would exceed their *local* competence were they to attempt to act as local confessors in Latin churches or oratories. Such confessions would be invalid unless the confessors had received express faculties from the proper ordinary who has exclusive jurisdiction over these sacred places.[32]

Difficulties concerning this particular interritual problem arose in Greece quite recently. The Latin Metropolitan of Athens proposed the following question to the Congregation for the Oriental Church: *"Can a priest of another rite and of another jurisdiction hear confessions and absolve validly and lawfully in a Latin church or oratory even though the Oriental ordinary who has approved him has jurisdiction in the territory of the Latin Archdiocese of Athens?"* The Sacred Congregation in its response declared that an Oriental priest who has been approved to hear confessions by an ordinary of his own

[31] Cf. *supra*, pp. 14-16.

[32] Personal jurisdiction is not thus restricted. The local and personal extent of personal jurisdiction will be discussed fully in Chapter IV.

rite cannot use that power *validly and lawfully* in territories and places which are under the exclusive jurisdiction of another ordinary of a different rite unless the latter ordinary has expressly given him the faculty to do so. A priest of the Greek-Byzantine rite who is approved by his own ordinary to hear confessions cannot *validly and lawfully* absolve in a church or oratory which is subject to the exclusive jurisdiction of an ordinary of the Latin rite unless the latter has expressly given him the faculties to do so.[33]

Upon the request of the Sacred Congregation for the Oriental Church the Sacred Congregation for the Propagation of the Faith instructed priests of the Latin rite in Greece through the Latin Metropolitan of Athens that they could not *validly and lawfully* hear confessions in a church or oratory which was under the exclusive jurisdiction of the ordinary of the Greek-Byzantine rite unless the latter had given them express faculties to do so.[34] Consequently interritual confessors in the United States and Canada must beware of exceeding the limits of the local jurisdiction which they possess, in order to avoid the danger of exercising their power unlawfully and invalidly.[35]

Article 2. Confessors Subject to Local Ordinaries of the Latin Rite

A. *Confessors of the Latin Rite*

By common law the following ecclesiastics have ordinary local jurisdiction in the internal sacramental forum: (1) Local Ordinaries [36] and canons penitentiary,[37] within the limits of their ecclesiastical circumscriptions; (2) pastors, within the limits of their

[33] S. C. Or., litt. (A. S. Ecc. Revm̃a il Segretario della S. C. de Prop. Fide), 26 aug. 1932—*Sylloge Praecipuorum Documentorum Recentium Summorum Pontificum et S. Congregationis de Propaganda Fide necnon aliarum SS. Congregationum Romanarum* (Romae: Typis Polyglottis Vaticanis, 1939), n. 173 (hereafter cited *Sylloge*). Italics appear in original.

[34] S. C. de Prop. Fide, litt. (A Mons. Giuseppe Cesarini, Sostituto della S. C. per Chiesa Orientale), 2 dec. 1932—*Sylloge*, n. 175.

[35] Cf. *supra*, p. 41.

[36] Canon 198, § 1.

[37] Canons 398 and 401.

parochial territory.[38] Quasi-pastors [39] and parochial vicars with full parochial power are in law considered equivalent to pastors.[40] The parochial vicar in charge of a church whose pastoral title is vested in a moral person,[41] administrators,[42] the substitute vicar (*substitutus*) [43] and the adjutant vicar (*adiutor*) who actually replaces the pastor in everything [44] are the parochial vicars commonly considered as having full parochial power.[45]

Common law does not give pastors local jurisdiction outside their parochial boundaries. Long before the promulgation of the Code there existed in most places the accepted usage whereby pastors were considered as having delegated jurisdiction for the whole diocese.[46] The Code has not abrogated this custom. In those places where it still prevails it may be considered as a valid source of delegated jurisdiction.[47] In the United States and Canada, however, pastors and their parochial equivalents generally do not depend on this custom as the source of their delegated local jurisdiction in the diocese. They usually possess diocesan faculties. These faculties give them delegated local jurisdiction to hear confessions in the whole diocese.[48] Pastors and their parochial equivalents in the Latin rite, therefore, possess in these countries an ordinary local

[38] Canon 873, §§ 1-2.

[39] Canon 216, § 3.

[40] Canon 451, § 2.

[41] Canon 471.

[42] Canons 472, 1° and 2°; 473, § 1.

[43] Canons 465, 474.

[44] Canon 475, § 2.

[45] Cf. Cappello, *De Poenitentia*, n. 385; Vermeersch-Creusen, *Epitome*, I, nn. 560-568; Coronata, *De Sacramentis*, I, n. 349b; Kelly, *The Jurisdiction of the Confessor*, pp. 46-47; Noldin-Schmitt, *Summa Theologiae Moralis iuxta Codicem Iuris Canonici* (26. ed., 3 vols., Oeniponte-Lipsiae: Rauch, 1939), III, n. 341 (hereafter cited *Summa Theologiae Moralis*).

[46] Cf. Cappello, *ibidem*, n. 384, 4; Kelly, *op. cit.*, p. 45; Motry, *Diocesan Faculties According to the Code of Canon Law*, p. 92; Vermeersch-Creusen, *op. cit.*, II, n. 144; Noldin-Schmitt, *loc. cit.*

[47] Cf. Cappello, *loc. cit.*; Motry, *loc. cit.*; Kelly, *op. cit.*, pp. 45-46; Vermeersch-Creusen, *loc. cit.*; Noldin-Schmitt, *loc. cit.*

[48] Motry, *op. cit.*, p. 93; cf. Faculties of the various archdioceses and dioceses, e.g., the Archdioceses of Washington, New York, Detroit, etc.

jurisdiction for the territory of their parishes and usually a delegated local jurisdiction for the rest of the diocese.

All other confessors of the Latin rite must receive local jurisdiction by way of delegation from the ordinary of the place where the confessions are heard.[49] The latter has the right to limit such delegated jurisdiction according to his prudent judgment.[50] Depending on circumstances he may grant delegated local jurisdiction for the internal sacramental forum to be exercised in all or in part of the territory committed to his care. The local extent of all delegated jurisdiction will necessarily depend on the terms of the grant. Usually in this country secular and religious priests engaged in the sacred ministry receive the faculties of the diocese in which they are performing their sacred duties. These faculties usually include delegated local jurisdiction to hear confessions in the whole diocese.[51]

All these local confessors of the Latin rite have explicit approval to administer the sacrament of penance within the scope of their local jurisdiction to any penitent of the Oriental rites who approaches their local tribunal. Churches and oratories which are under the exclusive jurisdiction of the Ruthenian ordinaries in the United States and Canada are from a juridic point of view outside the local competence of the local Latin ordinaries.[52] Consequently the local confessional jurisdiction which proceeds from the local Latin ordinaries cannot be validly or lawfully exercised in such churches or oratories.[53] In all other churches or oratories which

[49] Canon 874, § 1.

[50] Canon 878.

[51] E.g., in the Archdiocese of Washington, D. C.: *Facultates Quae Concedi Solent Sacerdotibus Qui in Archidioecesi Washingtoniensi Laborantes Nulli tamen Paroeciae Adscribuntur:* "Auctoritate nostra ordinaria, et etiam Apostolica Nobis a Summo Pontifice delegata, sequentes tibi in Domino concedimus facultates, ubivis per nostram Archidioecesim valituras usque ad revocationem, vel usquedum domicilium (aut saltem quasi-domicilium) intra fines huius Archidioecesis habere cessaveris:

1. Praedicandi Verbum Dei, et administrandi Sacramenta Baptismi, Eucharistiae, Poenitentiae et Extremae Unctionis (servatis servandis, praesertim Parochorum iuribus)."

[52] Cf. *supra*, p. 16.

[53] Cf. *supra*, pp. 40-42.

fall within the field of their local competence the Latin confessors can validly exercise their local jurisdiction. To exercise their power lawfully they must have the proper permission whenever ecclesiastical law requires it.[54]

B. Confessors of the Oriental Rites

All non-Ruthenian priests of the Oriental rites who are engaged in the sacred ministry in the United States and Canada are subject to the jurisdiction of the local Latin ordinaries. This includes Oriental priests who come from the territories of the Oriental rites [55] as well as those who were born in this country and have become incardinated in Latin dioceses.[56] The residential Latin bishops are their immediate pastors [57] and have the right to govern them in spiritual and temporal affairs with legislative, judicial and coercive episcopal power.[58] Normally the Latin bishops in the exercise of their episcopal power must be guided by the law of the Latin Code. They must be further mindful of the particular decrees and instructions of the Sacred Congregation for the Oriental Church, since it has jurisdiction in all matters which pertain to members of the Oriental rites.[59]

In recent years this Sacred Congregation has issued several important documents which contain detailed regulations concerning Oriental priests and clerics in North America. The decree *Qua sollerti,* promulgated on December 23, 1929, was enacted for the guidance of non-Ruthenian clerics of the Oriental rites who come to North America to care for the souls of the faithful of their rite.[60] Another decree, *Non raro accidit,* was issued on January 7, 1930, for the proper direction of the same Oriental clerics who come to North America for purposes other than the care of souls of the faithful of

[54] Cf. *supra,* p. 40.

[55] S. C. Or., decr. *Qua sollerti,* 23 dec. 1929, nn. 11, 17—*AAS,* XXII (1930), 99-105; Bouscaren, *Digest,* I, 17-24; instr., 26 sept. 1932, nn. 2, 5—*AAS,* XXIV (1932), 344-346; Bouscaren, *ibid.,* pp. 39-42.

[56] Cf. Diederichs, *The Jurisdiction of Latin Ordinaries Over Their Oriental Subjects,* p. 68.

[57] Canon 334, § 1.

[58] Canon 335, § 1.

[59] Canon 257.

[60] *AAS,* XXII (1930), 99-105; Bouscaren, *Digest,* I, 17-24.

their rite.[61] A later instruction, while it confirmed these two decrees, at the same time contained special prescriptions for all Oriental clerics who were living outside their own patriarchates or Oriental territories.[62] Consequently the residential bishops of the Latin rite in North America and the Oriental clerics concerned must obey these regulations in the concession of jurisdiction for the internal sacramental forum as well as in its use.[63]

According to these recent regulations the Sacred Congregation for the Oriental Church alone has the right to give non-Ruthenian priests of the Oriental rites the permission to come to North America for the care of souls. The Sacred Congregation sends written copies of the permission to the priests concerned and also to the ordinary of the diocese where such Oriental priests intend to establish their domicile.[64] On arrival the priests must present themselves to the ordinary of the diocese in which they are to exercise the sacred ministry. They are further obliged to show him the testimonial letter which they have received from the Sacred Congregation for the Oriental Church together with the letter in which their own bishop or patriarch grants them an authorized departure. The local ordinary is thereupon instructed to grant them permission to celebrate mass or the divine liturgy, to administer the sacraments and to perform all the sacred functions as well as to take up headquarters for the spiritual care of the faithful of their rite.[65]

Residential bishops in the United States and Canada are forbidden to admit indiscriminately to their dioceses non-Ruthenian priests who have come from the Oriental dioceses. They are not to permit such priests to say mass or to exercise the sacred ministry unless a special rescript has been sent from the Sacred Congregation of the Oriental Church.[66] No non-Ruthenian priest of an Oriental

[61] S. C. Or.—*AAS,* XXII (1930), 106-108; Bouscaren, *Digest,* I, 24-26.

[62] S. C. Or., 26 sept. 1932—*AAS,* XXIV (1932), 344-346; Bouscaren, *op. cit.,* I, 39-42.

[63] S. C. Or., *instr. cit.,* n. 9—*AAS,* XXIV (1932), 346; Bouscaren, *op. cit.,* I, 42.

[64] Decr. *Qua sollerti,* 23 dec. 1929, nn. 7-8—*AAS,* XXII (1930), 103; Bouscaren, *op. cit.,* I, 21.

[65] *Decr. cit.,* n. 10—*AAS,* XXII (1930), 103-104; Bouscaren, *op. cit.,* I, 22.

[66] *Ibidem,* n. 15—*AAS,* XXII (1930), 104-105; Bouscaren, *op. cit.,* I, 23.

rite may exercise the sacred ministry, even incidentally, in the dioceses of North America unless he has been admitted to the diocese for that purpose, or except at the command or with the express consent of the local ordinary.[67]

Before granting Oriental priests jurisdiction to hear confessions the local Latin ordinary has the right to judge their fitness by means of an examination if necessary.[68] He can also place certain restrictions on their exercise of the sacred ministry within his diocese. He can designate certain churches, parishes or localities within the diocese in which they are to exercise their sacred ministry. He may forbid them to exercise their powers in any other church, parish or locality.[69]

These non-Ruthenian Oriental priests are forbidden to go to another diocese for the temporary exercise of the sacred ministry, or to visit the faithful of their own rite, unless they have the previous consent of the bishop whose diocese they leave and of the bishop whose diocese they enter.[70] The local Latin ordinary can also forbid them to hear confessions in English or in any other language with which they might not be conversant.[71] Unless the restrictions are evidently contrary to the common law or to the particular rite in question, non-Ruthenian Oriental confessors in the United States and Canada must observe them.[72] In a case of doubt the presumption is that the restrictions as imposed by the local Latin ordinary are valid.

The Holy See has made no special regulations for priests of

[67] S. C. Or., instr., 26 sept. 1932, n. 5—*AAS,* XXIV (1932), 345; Bouscaren, *op. cit.,* I, 41.

[68] Canon 877, § 1.

[69] S. C. Or., decr. *Qua sollerti,* n. 12—*AAS,* XXII (1930), 104; Bouscaren, *op. cit.,* I, 22.

[70] S. C. Or., *ibidem,* nn. 12, 17—*AAS,* XXII (1930), 104, 105; Bouscaren, *op. cit.,* 22, 23.

[71] S. C. de Prop. Fide, 17 mart. 1760 (C. G.): "Missionarios teneri quocumque iure esse instructos idiomate in quo confessiones excipiunt; et Praelati Missionum non permittant missionariis huiusmodi muneris exercitium nisi praevio examine, vel per se vel per alios faciendo, de eorum idoneitate sibi constiterit."—*Fontes,* n. 4531; *Coll. S.C.P.F.,* n. 427.

[72] S. C. Or., *loc. cit.*

the Oriental rites who have been born in this country. There is nothing to prevent young men of the Oriental rites who aspire to the priesthood from being incardinated in a Latin diocese.[73] Their proper bishop may lawfully ordain them with an indult from the Holy See.[74] Such priests, once they have been judged competent to hear confessions in a diocese, will receive their jurisdiction from the local ordinary.

Depending on the circumstances, all non-Ruthenian priests of the Oriental rites in this country who desire to exercise the sacred ministry will be appointed either as pastors with the care of souls of the faithful of their rite within certain territorial limits or as assistant pastors. Those who are appointed pastors have in virtue of their office an ordinary jurisdiction in the internal sacramental forum over the faithful of their rite who are committed to their care. The jurisdiction of those confessors who are appointed as parochial assistants will depend upon the terms of the delegation.

Unless the contrary is expressed, all these confessors who have received ordinary or delegated jurisdiction may lawfully presume that they have *local* jurisdiction to hear confessions in the churches, oratories and other places designated by the local ordinary as the places in which they are to exercise the sacred ministry. If the local ordinary has extended to them the faculties of the diocese, they have delegated *local* jurisdiction to hear confessions in the whole diocese.[75] Within their local competence the non-Ruthenian confessors of the Oriental rites under Latin ordinaries in the United States and Canada may and should absolve all penitents, irrespective of rite, who approach their local tribunal.[76]

Article 3. Confessors Subject to Ruthenian Ordinaries

Each Ruthenian ordinary or apostolic exarch in the United States and Canada possesses full episcopal jurisdiction over the members

[73] Cf. Diederichs, *The Jurisdiction of Latin Ordinaries Over Their Oriental Subjects*, p. 68.

[74] Canon 955, § 2.

[75] Cf. Chapter IV in which the extent of personal jurisdiction is discussed in detail.

[76] *Fonti*, Serie I, Fasc. VIII, p. 711.

of his rite who are confided to his care.[77] His episcopal jurisdiction extends to all churches, missions, schools, seminaries, orphanages and other institutions under his exclusive pastoral care.[78] Each Ruthenian ordinary is empowered to appoint a vicar general to assist him in the manifold duties of his episcopal office.[79] Both the Ruthenian ordinary and his vicar general have ordinary local jurisdiction in the internal sacramental forum in all those places which are under their exclusive care.

In the government of their ordinariate the Ruthenian ordinaries in the United States and Canada must be mindful of the common law of the Universal Church, the law of their rite and the particular law which has been enacted by the Holy See for the territory.[80] They must see that the rites and discipline peculiar to the Ruthenian Church are faithfully observed in their entirety.[81] They must be vigilant and guard against any abuses which may arise especially in the administration of the sacraments.[82] The particular laws which at present are in force in the United States and Canada explicitly state that the Ruthenian ordinaries alone have the right to appoint the rectors of churches and missions.[83]

In the event that the Ruthenian exarchs in the United States do not have a sufficient number of their own priests who have been educated in the United States to care for the souls confided to the

[77] Cf. *supra,* pp. 12-15.

[78] S. C. Or., decr. *Cum data fuerit,* 1 mart. 1929, art. 4-7, 11 and 37—*AAS,* XXI (1929), 152-159; Bouscaren, *Digest,* I, 6-16; decr. *Graeci-Rutheni ritus,* 24 maii 1930, art. 4-7, 11 and 43—*AAS,* XXII (1930), 346-354; Bouscaren, *op. cit.,* I, 29-39.

[79] *Ibidem,* art. 4—*AAS,* XXI (1929), 153 and *AAS,* XXII (1930), 347. Cf. Bouscaren, *op. cit.,* I, 8 and 30.

[80] Holoweckyj, *Fontes Iuris Canonici Ecclesiae Ruthenae* (Romae: Typis Polyglottis Vaticanis, 1932), pp. 1-6; *supra,* pp. 12-14.

[81] *Decr. cit.,* art. 3—*AAS,* XXI (1929), 153 and *AAS,* XXII (1930), 346. Cf. Bouscaren, *op. cit.,* I, 7 and 29.

[82] *Decr. cit.,* art. 5—*AAS,* XXI (1929), 153 and *AAS,* XXII (1930), 347. Cf. Bouscaren, *op. cit.,* I, 8 and 30.

[83] Decr. *Graeci-Rutheni ritus,* art. 18—*AAS,* XXII (1930), 349; *Cum data fuerit,* art. 15—*AAS,* XXI (1929), 155. This article was slightly modified for the United States in 1940—*AAS,* XXXIII (1941), 27; Bouscaren, *Digest,* II, 6-7.

ordinariate, they are directed to ask for priests from the bishops of their rite in Galicia, Hungary or Jugoslavia through the agency of the Sacred Congregation for the Oriental Church.[84] They are forbidden to entrust churches or missions to any Greek-Ruthenian priests who are not celibates or who have come to the United States on their own authority without having been either invited by one of the local Ruthenian bishops or sent by the Sacred Congregation for the Oriental Church.[85] Besides being bound by similar regulations the Ruthenian apostolic exarchs in Canada are permitted to ask the local Latin ordinaries to allow some of their priests who are ready to adopt the Greek-Ruthenian rite to assume charge of Ruthenian missions until other arrangements can be made.[86]

If appointments of rectors to Ruthenian churches or missions in the United States and Canada were made contrary to these provisions of the Holy See, they would be unlawful but valid.[87] The instrument therefore whereby priests, secular or religious, receive ordinary jurisdiction of the internal sacramental forum is their valid appointment as rector of a mission or a church under the jurisdiction of the Ruthenian ordinary.[88] The rectors of Ruthenian churches and missions may exercise their ordinary jurisdiction and hear confessions in all those places which have been confided to their parochial or quasi-parochial care. Since they also usually possess the faculties of the Ruthenian ordinariate, they consequently have delegated local jurisdiction for their entire ordinariate.

Other priests have no local jurisdiction to hear confessions in places subject to the exclusive jurisdiction of a Ruthenian ordinary

[84] Decr. *Cum data fuerit,* art. 12—*AAS,* XXI (1929), 155; Bouscaren, *op. cit.,* I, 10.

[85] *Loc. cit.*

[86] Decr. *Graeci-Rutheni ritus,* art. 14-15—*AAS,* XXII (1930), 349; Bouscaren, *op. cit.,* I, 32-33.

[87] Canon 11.

[88] "Qui parochialem Ecclesiam non obtinent, etiamsi Regulares fuerint, Confessiones ne audiant, sine Episcopi approbatione."—*Synodus Provincialis Ruthenorum habita in civitate Zamosciae anno MDCCXX* (3. ed., Romae, 1883), p. 87 (hereafter cited *Synodus Provincialis Zamostena*). The laws of this Synod were extended to the entire Ruthenian nation by Pope Pius VII in 1807—Holoweckyj, *Fontes Iuris Canonici Ecclesiae Ruthenae,* pp. 11 and 30.

unless they have received such delegated jurisdiction from him.[89] The Holy See has expressly forbidden the Ruthenian ordinaries in North America to give faculties for the administration of the sacraments to Ruthenian priests who have come to this country on their own authority without having been invited, or if they have not been sent by the Sacred Congregation for the Oriental Church.[90] Furthermore, the Ruthenian ordinaries must be guided by other special prescriptions of the Holy See if they are desirous of granting faculties to non-Ruthenian Oriental priests who have come from the territories of the Oriental rites.[91] Under certain conditions these same ordinaries are permitted and even directed to grant jurisdiction to priests of the Latin rite. In places where the faithful of the Greek-Ruthenian rite are without either a mission or a priest of their own rite the Ruthenian ordinary should communicate his jurisdiction to a priest of the Latin rite in the locality.[92] In each case the local ordinary of the Latin rite is to be notified of what has been done.[93]

These particular prescriptions of the Holy See and the very nature of the episcopal office make it evident that each Ruthenian ordinary is obliged to assure himself of the fitness of the priests to whom he wishes to give delegated jurisdiction for the internal sacramental forum. Once he has satisfied himself of a priest's canonical fitness, each Ruthenian ordinary may grant delegated local jurisdiction to be exercised in one, some or all the places subject to his exclusive jurisdiction.[94] The local and temporal extent of this

89 *Synodus Provincialis Zamostena, loc. cit.; Fonti,* Serie I, Fasc. XI, n. 153; cf. also *supra,* pp. 40-42, 44.

90 S. C. Or., decr. *Cum data fuerit,* art. 12—*AAS,* XXI (1929), 155; Bouscaren, *Digest,* I, 10; decr. *Graeci-Rutheni ritus,* art. 14-15—*AAS,* XXII (1930), 349; Bouscaren, *op. cit.,* I, 32-33.

91 Cf. S. C. Or., decr. *Qua sollerti,* 23 dec. 1929—*AAS,* XXII (1930), 99-105; Bouscaren, *Digest,* I, 17-24; decr. *Non raro accidit,* 7 ian. 1930—*AAS,* XXII (1930), 106-108; Bouscaren, *op. cit.,* I, 24-26; instr., 26 sept. 1932—*AAS,* XXIV (1932), 344-346; Bouscaren, *ibidem,* pp. 39-42.

92 Decr. *Cum data fuerit,* art. 19—*AAS,* XXI (1929), 156; Bouscaren, *op. cit.,* I, 11-12; decr. *Graeci-Rutheni ritus,* art. 21—*AAS,* XXII (1930), 350; Bouscaren, *ibidem,* p. 34.

93 *Loc. cit.*

94 Canon 199, § 1.

delegated jurisdiction will depend on the will of the particular ordinary as expressed in the grant of jurisdiction. Such jurisdiction is generally given for the whole ordinariate, but very often is given only for a definite period of time.[95]

All the confessors who have obtained ordinary or delegated local jurisdiction from a Ruthenian ordinary can hear confessions in all those places which fall within the scope of their local competence. In such places they are lawfully approved confessors. Consequently, penitents of any rite are free to approach their local tribunal.[96] The confessors are free to absolve penitents of any rite who confess to them in their local tribunals.[97]

However, the local jurisdiction which has been received from the local ordinaries of the Ruthenian rite does not extend to churches or oratories which are under the exclusive care and jurisdiction of the local ordinaries of the Latin rite.[98] Nor does the ordinary or delegated local jurisdiction which has been received from one Ruthenian local ordinary extend to churches or missions which are under the exclusive jurisdiction of another local ordinary of the Ruthenian rite.[99] Interritual confessors who exceed the limits of their local jurisdiction would exercise their power unlawfully and invalidly.[100]

[95] E.g., in the Ruthenian ordinariate of Philadelphia such delegation is frequently given for the period of one year. Cf. *Eparkhialne Visti* (Philadelphia, 1926—), XXIV (1949), 20-21.

[96] Canon 905; cf. also *supra*, pp. 31-34.

[97] Cf. *supra*, pp. 36-37.

[98] Cf. *supra*, pp. 14-16, 40-42.

[99] Cf. *supra*, pp. 12-14.

[100] Cf. *supra*, p. 41.

CHAPTER IV

THE INTERRITUAL CONFESSOR WITH PERSONAL JURISDICTION

Besides confessors with local jurisdiction there are others with personal jurisdiction. Of course, it is true that every confessor who actually pronounces valid sacramental absolution absolves a person and of necessity does so in some place or locality. It is likewise true that one and the same confessor may simultaneously possess both local and personal jurisdiction. However, one must not conclude from these possibly confusing facts that there exists no juridic distinction between the two types of jurisdiction of the internal sacramental forum.

Both in its general and in its particular legislation the Church recognizes the existence of these two distinct types of jurisdiction. The first paragraph of canon 881 of the Latin Code determines the personal competence of a confessor's ordinary or delegated *local* jurisdiction, while the second paragraph of the same canon states that a confessor's ordinary *personal* jurisdiction is without local limitations.[1] According to the norms laid down by the Sacred Congregation of the Consistory, military vicars and chaplains possess a strictly personal jurisdiction over the subjects entrusted to their care.[2]

The fundamental difference between these two types of confessional jurisdiction is that personal jurisdiction empowers a priest to hear the confessions of certain persons, whereas local jurisdiction authorizes a priest to pronounce sacramental absolution in a certain

[1] § 1. Omnes utriusque cleri sacerdotes ad audiendas confessiones approbati in aliquo loco, sive ordinaria sive delegata iurisdictione instructi, possunt etiam vagos ac peregrinos ex alia dioecesi vel paroecia ad sese accedentes, itemque catholicos cuiusque ritus orientalis, valide et licite absolvere.

§ 2. Qui ordinariam habent absolvendi potestatem, possunt subditos absolvere ubique terrarum.

[2] Cf. *Military Faculties for the Military Ordinariate of the United States of America*—Bouscaren, *Digest*, II, 587.

place or locality. Although the same confessor may simultaneously possess both types of jurisdiction, the extent of the one is not identical with the extent of the other.[3] Personal jurisdiction automatically creates, as it were, a superior-subject relationship between the confessor and the subjects assigned to him.[4] Such a juridic relationship in turn requires that such a confessor possess the necessary title. Now, if this title is the possession of an office to which personal jurisdiction over the subject is attached by law, then the confessor's jurisdiction may be called ordinary personal jurisdiction.[5]

On the other hand, if the title or source of the confessor's personal jurisdiction over the penitent is delegation from a competent ecclesiastical authority, his jurisdiction may be called delegated personal jurisdiction. When such delegated jurisdiction is acquired in virtue of a positive disposition of law it is generally designated as deriving *a iure*.[6] Ordinary personal jurisdiction which extends to all penitents is universal, whereas that which embraces only individual persons or groups of persons is particular.[7] Delegated personal jurisdiction may have both territorial and personal limitations.[8]

In many sections of the United States and Canada Catholics of the Latin and of the various Oriental rites dwell within the confines of the same diocese, city or town. It often happens in these localities that members of the Oriental rites are subject to the episcopal or parochial jurisdiction of clerics of the Latin rite.[9] In any section of these countries every priest may sometimes possess personal jurisdiction to hear the confession of a person who belongs to a rite other than his own.[10] Such interritual confessors with personal jurisdiction must know what persons are subject to their jurisdiction. They must also know the territorial extent of the power they possess. To discover the personal and local extent of the personal jurisdiction which an interritual confessor may perchance possess is the purpose

[3] Canon 881.

[4] Cf. Coronata, *Institutiones*, I, n. 282; Beste, *Introductio*, p. 218.

[5] Augustine, *Commentary*, IV, 286.

[6] Cf. *infra*, pp. 63-69.

[7] Kelly, *The Jurisdiction of the Confessor*, p. 6.

[8] Cf. *infra*, pp. 60-63.

[9] Cf. *supra*, pp. 10-12.

[10] Cf. *infra*, pp. 63-64.

of this chapter. Since a confessor's jurisdiction must be either ordinary or delegated, the personal and territorial extent of each of these types will be discussed in separate articles.

Article 1. Ordinary Personal Jurisdiction

The incumbents of various ecclesiastical offices possess ordinary personal jurisdiction in the sacred tribunal of penance. The Roman Pontiff and the cardinals possess such jurisdiction over all baptized persons.[11] Their personal jurisdiction to hear confessions extends to women religious as well and is therefore universal. All other ordinary personal jurisdiction is particular, for it is limited to certain persons or groups of individuals. Local ordinaries, pastors, quasi-pastors and others who are juridically considered equivalent to pastors [12] have ordinary personal jurisdiction in the confessional over all those baptized persons who possess a domicile or quasi-domicile [13] in their particular ecclesiastical circumscription.[14]

Personal ordinaries and pastors have similar jurisdictional power over all those who are juridically committed to their care because of rite, language, family, work or profession.[15] The exact extent of their personal jurisdiction will usually depend on the particular prescriptions of the competent ecclesiastical authority.[16] Canons

[11] Cf. canons 87; 218; 239, § 1, 1°, and 873, § 1.

[12] Cf. *supra*, p. 43.

[13] Cf. canon 92.

[14] Canons 94, § 1, and 873, § 1.

[15] Cf. canons 216, § 4, and 366, § 3; *Military Faculties for the Military Ordinariate of the United States of America*—Bouscaren, *Digest*, II, 586-628; Coronata, *De Sacramentis*, I, n. 349b; Prümmer, *Manuale Theologiae Moralis* (8. ed., 3 vols., Friburgi Brisgoviae: Herder & Co., 1935-1936), II, n. 410 (hereafter cited *Manuale*); Ciesluk, *National Parishes in the United States*, The Catholic University of America Canon Law Studies, n. 190 (Washington, D. C.: The Catholic University of America Press, 1944), p. 15.

[16] For example, the jurisdiction of the military vicar and the chaplains of the American Armed Forces "extends to: a) All men of the armed forces belonging to the Army, Navy and Air Force who are in the active military service of the Federal Government or particular States; b) The wives, children, relatives and servants of the men of the armed forces who reside in the same house with them; c) All civilians staying within the limits of the military reservation; d) All religious—both men and women—also others, even lay

penitentiary also have ordinary personal jurisdiction to hear the confessions of all the baptized members of their own diocese.[17] Finally, the superiors of exempt clerical religious institutes possess similar power, which extends to all who have juridic membership in the communities under their jurisdiction.[18]

The juridic subjects of the religious superior's confessional jurisdiction are the professed religious, novices, postulants and all those who reside night and day in the religious house because of work, education, health or hospitality.[19] The fact that one enters the religious house for any of these reasons with the intention of staying there for a full day is sufficient to enable him to be considered a subject of the religious superior's sacramental jurisdiction.[20]

Beste is of the opinion that those who reside in the religious house because of work, education, health or hospitality do not fall within the competence of a religious superior's confessional jurisdiction when they are actually outside the domain of the religious house.[21] Other authors hold that the religious superior's confessional jurisdiction over these subjects is strictly personal and can be exercised anywhere as long as the bond of subjection perdures.[22] Since this milder opinion seems to be sufficiently probable a confessor would be justified in making application of it in practical cases.[23]

persons, who are attached to military hospitals; e) All priests who are subjects of the military vicar, by reason of service with the armed forces."—Bouscaren, *Digest*, II, 587.

[17] Cf. canons 94, § 1; 401; and 873, § 2.

[18] Canons 873, § 2, and 875, § 1. Cf. also Coronata, *De Sacramentis*, I, n. 349d.

[19] Canons 875, § 1, and 514, § 1.

[20] Vermeersch-Creusen, *Epitome*, I, n. 632; Cappello, *De Poenitentia*, n. 431.

[21] *Introductio*, p. 340.

[22] ". . . iurisdictio Superiorum religiosorum est personalis et eousque extenditur quo eunt subditi et quousque durat subditorum subiectio. Ideo iurisdictio qua gaudent Superiores in alumnos convictores et postulantes, etiam ad tempus feriarum quo per aliquot dies alumnos in domo parentum commorari contingat, extenditur . . ." Coronata, *De Sacramentis*, I, n. 349d. Cf. also Cappello, *De Poenitentia*, nn. 431-432.

[23] Canon 209.

Since the power exercised in the internal sacramental forum is judicial in nature it ordinarily could not, according to strict canonical principles, be exercised outside one's own territory.[24] Canon 881, § 2, of the Latin Code stands, as it were, as an exception to this general principle, for it explicitly states that confessors who possess ordinary personal jurisdiction can absolve their subjects anywhere in the world. The sources of this canon indicate that the Church has enacted as universal law what had been the accepted customary practice. In the 17th century the Sacred Congregation of the Council declared that bishops could not forbid pastors from hearing their parishioners' confessions outside the parochial limits.[25] Not long afterwards the same Sacred Congregation decreed that pastors could hear the confessions of their parishioners even outside their diocese.[26] Moral theologians discussed the question, and their common opinion, which Pope Benedict XIV explicitly approved,[27] was that bishops and pastors could hear the confessions of their parishioners anywhere.[28] It is this common teaching, then, that the Church has incorporated into its present written law.

All confessors of the Latin rite who possess ordinary personal jurisdiction can certainly hear the confessions of their subjects anywhere in the world in virtue of canon 881, § 2. They can validly exercise this power over their subjects in any land, on the sea and in the air, and even in churches and oratories of the Oriental rites. Unless the contrary is explicitly stated, the presumption is that particular laws which forbid Latins to hear confessions in churches or oratories of the Oriental rites under pain of nullity[29] refer to the exercise of local jurisdiction.[30]

But what of confessors of the Oriental rites who possess ordinary

[24] Canon 201, § 1.

[25] *Burgi S. Sepulchri*, 20 sept. 1698, ad 3, 4—*Fontes*, n. 2966.

[26] S. C. C., *Posnanien.*, 19 nov., 3 dec. 1707, ad 1—*Fontes*, n. 3058.

[27] Ep. encycl. *Apostolicum ministerium*, 30 maii 1753, § 22—*Fontes*, n. 425.

[28] Cf. De Lugo, *Disputationes Scholasticae et Morales* (2. ed., 8 vols., Parisiis, 1868-1869), IV, disp. 12, n. 8 (hereafter cited *Disputationes*).

[29] Cf. *supra*, pp. 41-42.

[30] Canon 23. In dubio revocatio legis praeexsistentis non praesumitur, sed leges posteriores ad priores trahendae sunt et his, quantum fieri possit, conciliandae.

personal jurisdiction? It is certain that cardinals of the Oriental rites can hear the confession of any baptized person anywhere, irrespective of the penitent's rite. This privilege is personal and is granted to all cardinals irrespective of the rite to which they belong.[31] It is likewise certain that priests of the various Oriental rites who are serving as chaplains in the American Armed Forces can anywhere absolve those who are entrusted to their care.[32] Such chaplains of the Oriental rites can therefore absolve their subjects anywhere irrespective of their rite.

Oriental ordinaries and pastors also have ordinary personal jurisdiction to hear the confessions of those who are entrusted to their care. May they also absolve their subjects anywhere? It is quite possible that ordinaries and pastors of the Oriental rites have adopted the common teaching and practice of the Latin Church in this matter, since they depend to a great extent on the conclusions of Latin moral theologians. Although there are particular laws of certain Oriental rites which contain prohibitive prescriptions relative to the hearing of confessions outside one's own diocese,[33] it is not clear that the prohibitions refer to ordinary personal as well as to local jurisdiction. In the absence of a law standing certainly to the contrary, the adoption of the practice of the Latin Church in this particular matter seems justifiable and in keeping with general canonical principles.[34]

[31] Canons 1 and 239, § 1, 1°.

[32] *Military Faculties for the Military Ordinariate of the United States of America*, n. 3: "[Jurisdictio Vicarii Castrensis et suorum Cappellanorum] amplectitur potestatem paroecialem quoad suos proprios subditos."—Bouscaren, *Digest*, II, 586.

[33] E. g., *Synodus Montis Libani (1736)* pars II, cap. 4, n. 6: "Ut parochi et confessarii possint extra dioecesim confessiones audire indigere decernimus peculiari facultate Rev.mi D. Patriarchae aut alterius Ordinarii vel parochi in cuius dioecesi versantur."—Mansi, XXXVIII, 53.

[34] Canon 20. Si certa de re desit expressum praescriptum legis sive generalis sive particularis, norma sumenda est, nisi agatur de poenis applicandis, a legibus latis in similibus; a generalibus iuris principiis cum aequitate canonica servatis, a stylo et praxi Curiae Romanae; a communi constantique sententia doctorum. Cf. Cappello, *Summa Iuris Canonici* (3 vols., Vol. I, Romae: Apud Aedes Universitatis Gregorianae, 1928), I, nn. 61-62 (hereafter cited *Summa Iuris Canonici*).

ARTICLE 2. DELEGATED PERSONAL JURISDICTION

The source of delegated jurisdiction is the competent ecclesiastical authority. Usually delegation proceeds from the person of the delegator to the person of the delegate. However, it need not always proceed directly from a physical person in this way. Delegation may and sometimes does proceed from a disposition of law in virtue of which the delegate acquires the power and authority to act.[35] To distinguish this latter type of jurisdiction from that which proceeds from the physical person of the delegator many authors refer to it as delegation which derives *a iure*.[36] The interritual confessor may acquire delegated personal jurisdiction in either of these two ways. Each type will therefore be discussed under its own separate heading.

A. *From the Physical Person of the Delegator*

A general principle of delegation states that one who possesses ordinary jurisdiction may delegate it in whole or in part.[37] Exceptions to this general principle are expressly made regarding the delegation of jurisdiction to hear confessions. Not all ecclesiastics who have ordinary jurisdiction to hear confessions have also the right to delegate their power to others. Cardinals,[38] pastors [39] and canons penitentiary [40] cannot delegate their ordinary jurisdiction of the internal sacramental forum to others. By the common law local ordinaries and superiors of exempt clerical religious institutes alone are empowered to grant delegated jurisdiction to hear confessions.[41] Special faculties, particular laws or privileges sometimes

[35] Kearney, *The Principles of Delegation*, The Catholic University of America Canon Law Studies, n. 55 (Washington, D. C.: The Catholic University of America, 1929), p. 60

[36] Coronata, *Institutiones*, I, n. 287; Cappello, *De Poenitentia*, n. 400; Vermeersch-Creusen, *Epitome*, I, n. 314, 2; Noldin-Schmitt, *Summa Theologiae Moralis*, III, n. 339; *et alii.*

[37] Canon 199, § 1.

[38] Cf. Vermeersch-Creusen, *Epitome*, II, n. 147.

[39] P. C. I., 16 oct. 1919, ad 3—*AAS*, XI (1919), 477; Bouscaren, *Digest*, I, 411.

[40] Canon 401, § 1.

[41] Canons 874, § 1 and 875, § 1.

give other ecclesiastics the right to delegate personal jurisdiction for hearing confessions.[42]

Local ordinaries can delegate confessional jurisdiction to any worthy priest, secular or religious, Latin or Oriental.[43] Although most priests in the United States and Canada usually have diocesan faculties which give them local jurisdiction to hear confessions in the whole diocese,[44] local ordinaries are not obliged to grant such faculties to all priests in the diocese. They have the right to give delegated confessional jurisdiction with local or personal limitations.[45] Thus they are free to appoint priests, though these do not possess diocesan faculties, as confessors to boarding schools, orphanages, hospitals or other pious institutions. Usually confessors may presume that their delegated jurisdiction is local unless the contrary is expressed.[46]

If the contrary is expressed, they will have merely a personal jurisdiction over the penitents committed to their care. Although the Latin Code warns against unreasonable restrictions, local or personal, in the delegation of jurisdiction for the hearing of confessions, it does not take away from ordinaries the power to make such unreasonable restrictions.[47] As a result confessors possessing merely a delegated personal jurisdiction who exceed the personal or local limits of their power act unlawfully and invalidly.[48]

[42] E. g., *Military Faculties for the Military Ordinariate of the United States of America*, pars I, *Index Facultatum Semper Vigentium: Quoad Sacramentum Poenitentiae*, n. 15: "Subdelegandi . . . ad confessiones excipiendas omnium subditorum Vicarii Castrensis, sed solummodo per modum actus, quemvis sacerdotem alienum, qui in propria sua dioecesi facultatibus ordinariis praeditus cognoscitur, vel si sit religiosus, qui a suis Superioribus approbatus est ad confessiones audiendas."—Bouscaren, *Digest*, II, 594.

[43] Canon 874, § 1.

[44] Cf. *supra*, pp. 43-44.

[45] Canon 878, § 1.

[46] Cappello, *De Poenitentia*, n. 395.

[47] Cf. Woywod-Smith, *A Practical Commentary on the Code of Canon Law* (2 vols., New York: Joseph F. Wagner, Inc., 1948), I, n. 404 (hereafter cited *A Practical Commentary*).

[48] Canon 203, § 1. Delegatus qui sive circa res sive circa personas mandati sui fines excedit, nihil agit.

The law of the Oriental [49] as well as of the Latin Church [50] ordinarily requires a priest to have special delegated personal jurisdiction in order to pronounce valid sacramental absolution in favor of women religious and novices. Although special jurisdiction is not required for hearing the confessions of postulants in religious institutes of women,[51] it is required for the granting of absolution in favor of women who live the common life in societies whose members do not take vows.[52] The Roman Pontiff and the cardinals do not need this special jurisdiction, for their ordinary personal jurisdiction of the internal sacramental forum is universal, so that it extends also to all women religious and novices throughout the world.[53]

Local ordinaries who have the right to give priests a delegated personal jurisdiction over women religious and novices in their territory naturally can also themselves hear the confessions of these penitents.[54] All other priests, secular or religious, Latin or Oriental, must obtain a special jurisdiction for hearing the confessions of women religious from the local ordinary in whose territory the religious house is located.[55] This specifically delegated personal jurisdiction may be either general or special according as it extends to all the women religious in the territory or to only those of a particular house or institute.[56]

Superiors of exempt clerical religious institutes have a cumulative right, which they share with local ordinaries, to delegate priests to hear the confessions of those who have juridic membership in the communities under their jurisdiction.[57]

[49] *Fonti*, Serie I, Fasc. XI, 146 and 451; Fasc. XII, nn. 345-346, 353; Coussa, *Epitome*, II (Typis Polyglottis Insulae S. Lazari, 1941), n. 41; Petrani, *De Relatione Iuridica inter Diversos Ritus*, p. 89.

[50] Canon 876, § 1.

[51] Coronata, *Institutiones*, I, n. 546.

[52] Canon 675. Cf. also Cappello, *De Poenitentia*, n. 437, 2.

[53] Cf. *supra*, p. 55.

[54] Augustine, *Commentary*, IV, 268.

[55] Canon 876, § 2; S. C. de Prop. Fide (C. G.), 11 dec. 1838, ad 9—*Fontes*, n. 4778; *Fonti*, Serie I, Fasc. XI, n. 146; Fasc. XII, 960; Coussa, *op. cit.*, II, n. 47; Petrani, *loc. cit.*

[56] Cappello, *op. cit.*, n. 440, 3; Coronata, *loc. cit.*

[57] Canon 876, § 1. Cf. also Coronata, *De Sacramentis*, I, n. 349; *supra*, pp. 55-56.

The major superiors of such institutes have this power of delegation.[58] The constitutions of the religious institutes may also acknowledge the same power to other superiors.[59]. Thus it is that Augustinian, Dominican and Carmelite local superiors have this power while Franciscan local superiors do not possess it.[60] Usually these religious superiors delegate the jurisdiction over their subjects directly by designating priests as confessors of the institute or of a particular house. They may also delegate the jurisdiction indirectly by giving the professed and novices the faculty of choosing any priest to hear their confessions.[61]

In the United States and Canada there are local Ordinaries of the Ruthenian as well as of the Latin rite.[62] There are also houses of exempt clerical religious institutes of the Ruthenian [63] as well as of the Latin rite. Oriental and Latin superiors have the right to delegate their ordinary personal jurisdiction to any worthy priest, even though he belongs to a rite other than their own. Although other reasons may sometimes dictate against it, there is no ecclesiastical law which prohibits the concession of delegated jurisdiction for hearing confessions to a priest in consequence simply of the diversity of his rite. However, in the granting of such delegations to priests of the Oriental rites both the Latin and the Ruthenian ordinaries must keep in mind the particular prescriptions of the Holy See as well as the laws of their own rite.[64] According to their prudent judgment therefore Latin ordinaries can lawfully appoint worthy priests of the Oriental rites as confessors for religious houses of men or women, and also for boarding schools, hospitals, orphanages or other pious institutions under their jurisdiction.[65] Ruthenian ordi-

[58] Cf. Cappello, *op. cit.*, n. 386; Beste, *Introductio*, p. 339.

[59] Canons 873, § 2, and 875, § 1.

[60] Clancy, *The Local Religious Superior* (The Catholic University of America Canon Law Studies, n. 175, Washington, D. C.: The Catholic University of America Press, 1943), pp. 145-146.

[61] Beste, *op. cit.*, p. 340.

[62] Cf. *supra*, pp. 12-16.

[63] Cf. *The Official Catholic Directory (1949)*, Part II, pp. 603, 607; Part III, pp. 117-120.

[64] Cf. *supra*, pp. 45-52.

[65] Diederichs, *Jurisdiction of the Latin Ordinaries over Their Oriental Subjects*, p. 97.

naries may for the hearing of the confessions of their subjects similarly give delegated personal jurisdiction to worthy priests of the Latin rite.[66]

The personal extent of the delegated personal jurisdiction of these confessors will depend upon the personal limitations expressed in the act or instrument of delegation.[67] The local extent of such jurisdictional power will vary by reason of its nature and source. Thus the delegated jurisdiction received from the superiors of exempt clerical institutes over the professed, novices and those who reside in the religious house because of work, education, health or hospitality is strictly personal and has no local limitations.[68]

On the other hand, unless the contrary is expressed, the delegated personal jurisdiction received from local ordinaries can be exercised anywhere within the limits of the ordinariate, but not beyond its local boundaries.[69] Penitents are always free to confess their sins to confessors who have delegated personal jurisdiction over them, and confessors can lawfully and validly absolve these penitents within the local and personal field of their personal jurisdiction even though a diversity of rite exists between them.[70]

B. *From Positive Dispositions of the Law*

To provide for the spiritual needs of certain individuals or groups the supreme legislator, sometimes by means of positive and express dispositions of the law, grants priests jurisdiction to hear the confessions of certain persons. Baptized persons in danger of death are provided for in this way. Ecclesiastical law expressly states that every validly ordained priest is empowered to absolve any baptized person in danger of death.[71]

It makes no difference what the present status of the priest may be. Though he be degraded or laicized, in communion or out of communion with the Church, every priest automatically possesses

66 Cf. *supra*, pp. 50-51.

67 Canons 203, § 1; 878, § 1; and 879, § 1.

68 Cf. *supra*, p. 56.

69 Cf. canon 881, § 2; Vermeersch-Creusen, *Epitome*, II, n. 151.

70 Canon 905. Cf. *supra*, pp. 28-34.

71 Conc. Trident., sess. XIV, *de poenitentia*, c. 7; canon 882.

personal jurisdiction to absolve the penitent as long as the danger lasts.[72] It likewise does not make any difference whether the cause of the danger is intrinsic or extrinsic.[73] Although no penitent is excluded from the valid use of this extensive power, there is however one personal restriction placed on its lawful use. Even in the presence of the danger of death a priest, Latin or Oriental, is forbidden to absolve his accomplice ***in peccato turpi*** except in a case of necessity.[74] While the sacramental absolution pronounced contrary to this prohibition would be valid, the priest who would absolve such a penitent when another priest is available commits a serious sin and incurs a severe censure.[75]

In the past the question of just who had ordinary jurisdiction to hear the confessions of bishops and other prelates caused some discussion among canonists and moral theologians. Some were of the opinion that in the sacred tribunal of penance bishops were subject to the ordinary jurisdiction of their archbishop, archbishops to that of their patriarch, and patriarchs to that of the Roman Pontiff.[76] Others held that bishops and other superior prelates were subject only to the ordinary jurisdiction of the Roman Pontiff in the sacred tribunal of penance.[77]

Pope Gregory IX (1227-1241), in view of the good of souls and of relieving such prelates from the necessity of always having recourse to their lawful superior, granted bishops and other superiors the privilege of confessing their sins to the confessor of their choice.[78]

[72] Cappello, *De Poenitentia*, n. 408; Kelly, *The Jurisdiction of the Confessor*, pp. 92-93.

[73] S. Poenit., 29 maii 1915—*AAS*, VII (1915), 282; Bouscaren, *Digest*, I, 411.

[74] Canons 882 and 884; Benedictus XIV, const. *Sacramentum poenitentiae*, 1 iun. 1741—*Documentum V in Codice*; S. C. de Prop. Fide, litt. encycl., 6 aug. 1885—*Fontes*, n. 4910.

[75] Canons 882, 884 and 2367. Cf. also Ayrinhac, *Legislation on the Sacraments in the New Code of Canon Law* (New York-London: Longmans, Green and Co., 1928), n. 176b (hereafter cited *Legislation on the Sacraments*).

[76] Cf. Pirhing, *Ius Canonicum* (5 vols., Dilingae, 1674-1678), lib. V, tit. 38, n. 23.

[77] Cf. De Lugo, *Disputationes*, IV, disp. 19, n. 2.

[78] C. 16, X, *de poenitentiis et remissionibus*, V, 38.

Even titular bishops enjoyed this privilege.[79] Moreover, bishops had the right to exempt, as it were, their household from the confessional jurisdiction of other prelates in such a way that a confessor selected by a bishop had jurisdiction to hear the confessions of the members of the episcopal household as well as that of the bishop.[80] Cardinals, by custom at least, enjoyed the same privilege as bishops.[81] The present written law of the Church whereby cardinals and bishops, even titular, are given the privilege of choosing a confessor for themselves and for the members of their household is therefore not a canonical innovation.[82]

According to the present discipline cardinals possess this privilege from the moment of their promotion in the Consistory,[83] while bishops receive it upon the official notification of their canonical provision.[84] These prelates may choose their confessors directly or indirectly, explicitly or implicitly.[85] The priests so chosen, even though they are otherwise without jurisdiction, automatically obtain personal jurisdiction to hear the confessions of the cardinals or of the bishops and of the members of their household.[86] All persons, cleric or lay, who live night and day with the cardinal or the bishop, such as secretaries, domestics, relatives or even consultors, are considered members of the household.[87] The confessors of cardinals and of bishops can anywhere absolve the penitents who are subject to their delegated personal jurisdiction, since their jurisdiction is strictly personal and not limited by territorial or geographical boundaries.[88]

Women religious who are seriously ill or who seek peace of conscience also have definite privileges in virtue of which they enjoy limited freedom in the choice of a confessor. Women religious of

79 Pirhing, *loc. cit.*

80 De Lugo. *op. cit.*, IV, disp. 19, n. 5.

81 De Lugo, *loc. cit.*

82 Canons 239, § 1, 2°, and 349, § 1, 1°.

83 Canon 233.

84 Canon 349, § 1.

85 Cf. Cappello, *De Poenitentia*, n. 400.

86 Canon 239, § 1, 2°.

87 Cappello, *loc. cit.*; Beste, *Introductio*, p. 235.

88 Canon 239, § 1, 2°. Cf. also Vermeersch-Creusen, *Epitome*, II, n. 151.

the Oriental rites as well as those of the Latin rite are the recipients of the benefits of these privileges.[89] Every woman religious who is seriously ill, though there be no danger of death, has the right to ask for and to confess her sins to any priest approved for the hearing of women's confessions. During her illness the religious can as often as she so desires, receive valid absolution from the priest so chosen.[90]

The Church requires the fulfillment of certain essential conditions in order that the sacramental absolution which is pronounced in virtue of this privilege be valid. The first essential condition is that the religious be seriously ill. An illness which causes grave physical discomfort or requires a surgical operation or could easily become dangerous is usually considered serious.[91] In the case of a religious an illness is also considered serious when it is such that a physician must be called [92] or when it will keep the patient in bed for a week or two.[93]

A relatively grave illness sufficiently fulfills this essential condition, for an illness which might not be considered serious for one woman religious might well be quite serious in the case of another.[94] Since the valid acquisition of this personal power to hear the confession of the sick religious depends rather on the confessor's prudent judgment that a serious illness is present than on the actual presence of such an illness, the sick religious must be given the benefit of the doubt in practice.[95]

The other essential condition is that the priest selected by the religious has jurisdiction for hearing the confessions of women.[96] It is not necessary that he have general jurisdiction to hear the confession of *all* women, secular or religious; it is sufficient if he has approval for hearing the confessions of *some* women or of a group of

[89] Coussa, *Epitome*, II, nn. 44-45.

[90] Canon 523.

[91] Cappello, *op. cit.*, n. 454; Beste, *op. cit.*, p. 347; Vermeersch-Creusen, *Epitome*, I, n. 645.

[92] Woywod-Smith, *A Practical Commentary*, I, n. 404.

[93] Beste, *loc. cit.*; Kelly, *The Jurisdiction of the Confessor*, p. 206.

[94] Kelly, *loc. cit.*

[95] Cappello, *op. cit.*, nn. 454-455.

[96] Canon 523.

women.[97] There is no doubt that, if a priest who has been called to hear the confession of the seriously ill woman religious has jurisdiction to hear the confessions of women from the ordinary of the place where the confession is being heard, he has the right to pronounce valid sacramental absolution. A few authors are also of the opinion that a priest who has approval for hearing the confessions of women from *any* local ordinary can validly and lawfully absolve in virtue of canon 523, even though he has not received jurisdiction from the ordinary of the place where the confession is being heard.[98] Beste holds, on the contrary, that this opinion lacks probability.[99]

For the peace of her conscience ecclesiastical law gives every woman religious the right to use any occasion that presents itself to confess her sins to any priest approved by the local ordinary for hearing the confessions of women.[100] The religious may make use of this privilege either inside or outside her religious house; she may even call or invite the confessor to the religious house for the very purpose of making use of her privilege.[101] This privilege is intended for occasional and not for habitual use.[102] For this reason the priest so chosen in such cases by a woman religious is generally called her *occasional* confessor.[103]

The privilege does not entitle women religious to absolute freedom in the choice of a confessor or of the place of the confession. It simply enables women religious to receive valid absolution from a priest who for hearing the confessions of women has jurisdiction from the ordinary of the place where the confession is heard. It is

97 Vermeersch-Creusen, *op. cit.*, I, n. 644.

98 Cf. McCormick, *Confessors of Religious*, The Catholic University of America Canon Law Studies, n. 33 (Washington, D.C.: The Catholic University of America, 1926), pp. 224-229; Kelly, *op. cit.*, p. 207.

99 *Introductio*, p. 347.

100 Canon 522.

101 P. C. I., 28 dec. 1927, ad II—*AAS*, XX (1928), 61; Bouscaren, *Digest*, I, 296

102 Cappello, *op. cit.*, n. 446. Cf. also *Letter of the Secretary of the Sacred Congregation of Religious to the Bishop of Osnabrück*, December 1, 1921—Bouscaren, *op. cit.*, I, 296-297.

103 Vermeersch-Creusen, *Epitome*, I, 644; Beste, *op. cit.*, p. 544.

sufficient that the priest have jurisdiction to hear the confessions of *some* women.[104] The legislator further requires that the religious make her confession in a church, in a semi-public or public oratory,[105] or in another place lawfully designated for the hearing of women's confessions,[106] be the women secular or religious.[107] A lawfully designated place is not only one that is permanently arranged for the confessions of women but also one that is temporarily and lawfully selected in particular and extraordinary cases.[108] Occasional confessions which do not satisfy these essential conditions as postulated in the law are not only illicit but invalid.[109]

These privileges give cardinals, bishops and women religious, within the limits postulated in the law, the right to choose priests to hear their confessions, and thus indirectly cause the priest so selected to obtain the necessary personal jurisdiction to absolve them. The designation or choice of the priest by the prelate or the woman religious gives the priest a personal jurisdiction to absolve in the event that he previously lacked jurisdiction over the prelate, the members of his household or the woman religious.[110]

The Holy See has explicitly declared that priests of the Oriental and of the Latin rites can act as occasional confessors of women religious, even though a diversity of rite exist between confessor and penitent.[111] Furthermore, the ecclesiastical laws which grant these privileges do not restrict cardinals, bishops or women religious to priests of their own rite in the use of their privileges. Consequently, it seems tenable to maintain that cardinals, bishops and seriously ill

[104] Cf. *supra*, p. 65.

[105] Canon 522

[106] P. C. I., 24 nov. 1920—*AAS*, XII (1920), 575; Bouscaren, *op. cit.*, I, 295.

[107] P. C. I., 28 dec. 1927, ad II—*AAS*, XX (1928), 61; Bouscaren, *op. cit.*, I, 296.

[108] P. C. I., 12 febr., 1935—*AAS*, XXVII (1935), 92 Bouscaren, *Digest*, II, 161.

[109] P. C. I., 24 nov. 1920—*AAS*, XII (1920), 575; Bouscaren, *Digest*, I, 295; 28 dec. 1927, ad I—*AAS*, XX (1928), 61; Bouscaren, *op. cit.*, I, 296.

[110] Woywod-Smith, *A Practical Commentary*, I, n. 403.

[111] S. C. de Religiosis, *Romana et Aliarum*, 3 maii 1914, ad I—*AAS*, VI (1914), 232.

women religious also have the right to select as their confessors priests who belong to a rite other than their own. The interritual confessors who receive delegated personal jurisdiction as a result of the use of these privileges must conform to the prescriptions of law as described in the preceding pages if they are to exercise their power lawfully and validly.

CHAPTER V

THE MATERIAL COMPETENCE OF THE INTERRITUAL CONFESSOR

THE interritual confessor must be familiar with the material as well as with the local and personal extent of his jurisdiction. Since the confessor as such possesses jurisdiction of the internal forum,[1] those matters which require the possession of jurisdiction of the external forum do not ordinarily fall within the scope of his material competence.[2] Consequently the confessor cannot normally dispense from matrimonial impediments, from irregularities, or from vindictive penalties.[3] Even his power to absolve from sin and censure not only can be but actually is limited materially in consquence of the reservations established by competent ecclesiastical superiors.[4]

Ecclesiastical law does, however, sometimes give the confessor extensive power whereby he is enabled to absolve and to dispense from matters ordinarily beyond his material competence.[5] The interritual confessor must therefore know what his material competence is. He must know to what extent it is limited in consequence of the reservations established by competent ecclesiastical superiors. He must know if and when he is empowered to dispense from matrimonial impediments, from irregularities, and from vindictive penalties. The purpose of the following articles is to discover the answers to these possibly perplexing problems which may confront the interritual confessor.

[1] Cf. *supra*, pp. 28-29.

[2] Canon 202, § 1.

[3] Cf. canons 1040; 990, § 1, and 2289; Coussa, *Epitome*, I, n. 261.

[4] Cf. *infra*, pp. 71-73.

[5] Cf. e.g. canons 882; 2252; 2254; 990, § 2; 1044; 1045, § 3; 2290; Pius XII, motu propr. *Crebrae allatae*, 22 febr. 1949, can. 33-35—*AAS*, XXXXI (1949), 96-97.

Article 1. Limitation of Material Competence

A. *The Nature of Reservation*

Because of its judicial character sacramental absolution requires in the minister the power of jurisdiction in addition to the power of Orders.[6] The power of Orders which is received in valid ordination is indivisible and inamissible, while the power of jurisdiction which is acquired through the lawful possession of an ecclesiastical office or in consquence of an act of delegation is both divisible and amissible.[7] The latter power, with the exception of the Roman Pontiff's unvarying possession of it, is partially or wholly divisible and amissible for the simple reason that it is a communicated power, which proceeds either directly or indirectly from lawful ecclesiastical authority.[8] Thus it is that the confessor's jurisdictional power to absolve from sin and censure, which is in itself general and unrestricted, can be materially limited in consequence of the reservations established by lawful ecclesiastical superiors.[9]

The term "reservation," as it is used here, designates the act whereby a competent superior limits to himself or to others the power to absolve from certain sins or censures.[10] The Roman Pontiff in virtue of his primacy of jurisdiction can enact reservations for the whole Church,[11] while residential bishops and those who possess the equivalent of episcopal jurisdiction enjoy the same prerogative within the limits of their respective circumscriptions.[12]

The direct object of a reservation may be either a sin or a censure. If its direct object is a censure which does not prevent the reception of the sacraments, the delinquent may receive sacramental absolution

[6] Cf. *supra*, pp. 28-29.

[7] Ayrinhac, *Legislation on the Sacraments*, n. 198.

[8] Ayrinhac, *loc. cit.*

[9] Cf. D'Annibale, *Summula Theologiae Moralis* (5. ed., 3 vols., Romae, 1908), I, n. 338, nota 16 (hereafter cited *Summula*).

[10] Cf. canon 893, § 1-2; also Stadalnikas, *Reservation of Censures*, The Catholic University of America Canon Law Studies, n. 208 (Washington, D. C.: The Catholic University of America Press, 1944), p. 19

[11] Conc. Trident., sess. XIV, *de poenitentia*, c. 7; canons 218 and 893, § 1.

[12] Conc. Trident., sess. XIV, *de poenitentia*, c. 7, can. 11; canons 874, § 1, and 893, § 1; Leo XIII, litt. ap. *Orientalium*, 30 nov. 1894, n. VI—*Fontes*, n. 627; Coussa, *Epitome*, I, n. 260.

though he remain under censure.[13] If, on the contrary, its direct object is a censure which impedes the reception of the sacraments, the delinquent cannot be absolved from the sin until the censure has been removed.[14] In this case the sin is the indirect object of the reservation and is said to be reserved by reason of the censure (*ratione censurae*).[15] If a sin is the direct and primary object of the reservation, it is said to be reserved in consideration of itself or *ratione sui*.[16]

There is a radical difference between the reservation of a sin and the reservation of a censure. Each has a distinct direct object.[17] The reservation of a sin *ratione sui* consists precisely in the positive act of a competent ecclesiastical superior whereby the sin, the direct object of the reservation, is withdrawn from the material competence of the confessors who are subjects of the superior. The power to absolve, which in and of itself is unrestricted, thereby becomes materially limited.[18]

The reservation of a censure has as its direct object a censure, even though sometimes because of its connection with the reserved censure the sin will become indirectly and secondarily reserved.[19] Now, a censure is an ecclesiastical penalty primarily of the external forum. It deprives the delinquent of certain benefits, be they spiritual in themselves or annexed to spiritual things.[20] The power to

[13] Canon 2250, § 1.

[14] Canon 2250, § 2.

[15] Canon 898. Cf. also Cappello, *De Poenitentia,* n. 508.

[16] Canon 894.

[17] Cappello, *op. cit.*, nn. 504 and 508; Ayrinhac, *Legislation on the Sacraments,* n. 202.

[18] ". . . iurisdictio absolvendi tum a peccatis (quae datur in sacra ordinatione), tum a censuris (quae profluit ab eo qui censuras invehit) generalis est; illa ex ordinatione ipsa, haec ex voluntate eius, qui censuram invexit (quia reservatio censurarum non intelligitur nisi fuerit expressa, C. Nuper, 29, De S. E. [=c. 29, X, *de sententia excommunicationis*, V, 39]) proficiscitur. Sed revera, iurisdictio per reservationem, illic adimitur, hic non datur."— D'Annibale, *Summula*, I, n. 338, nota 16. Cf. also Coronata, *Institutiones*, IV, n. 1749; Ayrinhac, *op. cit.*, n. 198.

[19] Cf. *supra*, p. 71.

[20] Canon 2241, § 1. Cf. also Ayrinhac, *Penal Legislation in the New Code*

absolve from a censure therefore primarily pertains to the external forum. However, for the good of souls it can also be exercised in the sacramental forum.[21]

Confessors did not always have the right to absolve from censures. Pope Innocent III (1198-1216) authorized their proper bishop or priest to absolve those penitents who had contracted a minor excommunication in consequence of their association with a person who was under a major excommunication. The proper bishop or priest was empowered to absolve in this case because the legislation had made no express mention of the reservation.[22] Although the Roman Pontiff had spoken only of minor excommunications enacted in the common law, canonists with the implicit approval of the legislator applied the same principle to all censures which were not expressly reserved.[23]

The present law states that censures incurred *ab homine* are reserved to the one who imposed them, to his superior, to his successor, or to his delegate,[24] whereas *latae sententiae* contracted censures are not reserved unless the law or the precept expressly declares the contrary.[25] Thus, although the confessor's power to absolve from censures is in and of itself general and unrestricted, it is actually limited in consequence of the reservations established by competent ecclesiastical superiors. However, the reservation of a censure limits the confessor's jurisdiction in a different way than does the reservation of a sin. The reservation of a sin consists in a positive act whereby power already possessed is withdrawn, while the reservation of a censure consists rather in a negative act whereby the necessary power to absolve from the censure has not been granted.[26]

of Canon Law (New York-Cincinnati-Chicago: Benziger Brothers, 1920), nn. 75-76 (hereafter cited *Penal Legislation*).

[21] D'Annibale, *op. cit.*, I, n. 336.

[22] C. 29, X, *de sententia excommunicationis*, V, 39.

[23] Cf. Coronata, *Institutiones*, IV, n. 1750; Ayrinhac, *op. cit.*, n. 84; Stadalnikas, *Reservation of Censures*, p. 14.

[24] Canon 2245, § 1.

[25] Canon 2245, § 4. Cf. also Stadalnikas, *op. cit.*, pp. 78-84.

[26] D'Annibale, *op. cit.*, I, n. 338, nota 16. Cf. *supra*, p. 72, footnote 18; Coronata, *Institutiones*, IV, n. 1756; Ayrinhac, *Legislation on the Sacraments*, n. 198.

B. *The Reservation to Which the Interritual Penitent is Subject*

The determining of the reservation to which the penitent is subject is of prime importance to an interritual confessor. This is especially true relative to those sins which are reserved indirectly by reason of the attached censure, for in such cases the sins are not reserved if the censures are not incurred.[27] Difficulties in the matter of determining the reservation to which the interritual penitent is subject will usually be concerned with censures which are reserved *a iure*. For this reason no special consideration will be given to *ab homine* reserved censures.

1. Penitents of the Latin Rite

The reservations to which the interritual penitent of the Latin rite is bound do not present great difficulty. Such a penitent is subject generally to two classes of reservations, namely, those which are contained in the enactments of particular and of universal law. The universal law of the Latin Church is contained in the Code. Consequently, a penitent of the Latin Rite is subject to the reservations enacted in the Code in proportion to his subjection to the law in which the reservations are established.[28] Of all the reservations enumerated in the Code there is mention in canon 894 of but a single sin which is reserved *ratione sui*. All other sins reserved in the general law of the Latin Church are reserved by reason of the attached censure.[29]

The territorial reservations of sin and censure in force in a particular locality may be as diverse as the sources of particular territorial law. These sources may be the Holy See,[30] plenary or provincial councils,[31] diocesan synods,[32] or other legislative acts of the residential bishops. Interritual penitents of the Latin rite in the United States and Canada will consequently be subject to the ter-

[27] Canon 2246, § 2.
[28] Cf. canons 12; 2226-2232.
[29] Cappello, *De Poenitentia*, n. 514, 3.
[30] Canon 82.
[31] Canons 290-291.
[32] Canon 362.

ritorial reservations of sin and censure according as they are subject to the law in which the reservations are established.[33]

2. Penitents of the Oriental Rites

The determining of the reservations to which the interritual penitents of the Oriental rites in the United States and Canada are subject is a more difficult matter. These Orientals are living outside their patriarchal or Oriental territory. Members of the Ruthenian rite are subject to their own ordinaries, while non-Ruthenian Orientals are subject to the residential bishops of the Latin rite.[34]

a. The Law of the Rite

All Oriental Catholics in this country retain their own rite.[35] They are obliged to observe the laws of their own rite, especially those which pertain to their personal status, their capacity, the divine worship and the liturgy.[36] The members of the Oriental rites are therefore subject to the reservations which are established in the law of their proper rite, since they remain bound by that law.[37] This does not mean that Orientals in the United States and Canada remain subject to the territorial reservations enacted for Oriental territory by patriarchal, national, plenary or provincial councils or by diocesan synods. They are not subject to these territorial reservations, for they have no residence in the Oriental territory in which exclusively these reservations have applicable force.[38]

33 Cf. canons 8; 13, § 2; 14; 900, 3°, and 2247, § 2.

34 Cf. *supra*, pp. 10-16.

35 Leo XIII, litt. ap. *Orientalium*, 30 nov. 1894, n. IX—*Fontes*, n. 627; canon 98, § 3.

36 Cf. Herman, "De 'Ritu' in Iure Canonico," *Orientalia Christiana* (Romae, 1922-1935; ab anno 1935: *Orientalia Christiana Analecta*, Romae 1935—) XXXII (1933), 153-157; Van Hove, *Commentarium Lovaniense in Codicem Iuris Canonici*, Vol. I, Tom. II, *De Legibus Ecclesiasticis* (Mechliniae-Romae: Dessain, 1930), p. 8; Cicognani, *Canon Law* (2. ed. trans. by J. O'Hara and F. Brennan, Westminster: The Newman Bookshop, 1947), pp. 450-456.

37 Cf. Cappello, *Tractatus Canonico-Moralis de Censuris* (2. ed., Taurinorum Augustae: Marietti, 1925), n. 22 (hereafter cited *De Censuris*); Duskie, *The Canonical Status of Orientals in the United States*, p. 133, footnote 34.

38 Canon 13, § 2; Herman, *loc. cit.*; Duskie, *loc. cit.*

b. The Law in the Territory

Members of the Oriental rites who have established their domicile in North America are subject to the reservations established in the territorial or territorial-personal jurisdictions to which they are now subject. Thus the reservations imposed by the ordinaries of the Ruthenian rite in the United States and Canada extend to those Ruthenians who are subject to their respective jurisdictions.[39] Non-Ruthenian Orientals are subject to the reservations enacted by the residential bishops of the Latin rite, who have full episcopal jurisdiction over them.[40]

The non-Ruthenian members of the Oriental rites may also be subject to the territorial reservations which are established by the local plenary or provincial councils. The enactments of these legislative bodies are presumably made for Catholics as members of the territory, since the particular legislative authority of such councils is of its nature territorial.[41]. Those who are subject to the territorial authority of the plenary or provincial councils are bound by their legislative enactments.[42] Since all non-Ruthenian Orientals in the United States and Canada are subject to the territorial jurisdiction of the local Latin ordinaries, they are also presumably bound by the reservations which are contained in the enactments of plenary or provincial councils, as are residents of the Latin rite.[43] However, they are not bound by those territorial reservations which are connected with matters prejudicial to their proper rite.[44]

c. The Law in the Latin Code

Although all non-Ruthenian Orientals in the United States and Canada are subject to the jurisdiction of the residential bishops of

[39] Cf. *supra*, pp. 12-14; also S. C. Or., decr. *Cum data fuerit*, 1 mart. 1929, art. 2, 31—*AAS*, XXI (1929), 152, 157; decr. *Graeci-Rutheni Ritus*, 24 maii 1930, art. 2, 36—*AAS*, XXII (1930), 346, 352.

[40] Cf. *supra*, pp. 10-12; canons 893, § 1; 2220-2221; Duskie, *op. cit.*, p. 138.

[41] Cf. canons 8, § 2 and 291, § 2.

[42] Canon 291, § 2.

[43] Cf. *supra*, pp. 74-75.

[44] Herman, "De 'Ritu' in Iure Canonico," *Orientalia Christiana*, XXXII (1933), 153-154.

the Latin rite, it must not be concluded that they are subject to all the reservations enumerated in the Latin Code.[45] It is true that these Orientals are members of Latin dioceses, but this fact does not make them members of the Latin Church.[46] They still retain their rite, and basically they are no more subject to the Latin Code than are the Ruthenians in these countries. Canon 1 expressly states that generally Orientals are not bound to observe the discipline of the Latin Church. The terms of the canon are general. No distinction is made therein between Orientals who are not subject to the jurisdiction of local Latin ordinaries and those who are. One is not justified in making unwarranted distinctions when the law itself abstains from doing so.[47] As a consequence Orientals in the United States and Canada are bound by the reservations enumerated in the Latin Code only in so far as they are included under the law of the Code by reason of canon 1.

This canon states that Orientals are subject to the law of the Code if they are expressly mentioned or are included from the very nature of the case (*ex ipsa rei natura*). Since Orientals are not expressly mentioned in any of the canons which pertain to reservations, it will be necessary to discover the meaning of the expression *ex ipsa rei natura* before any attempt can be made to extend to Orientals any reservations enumerated in the Code.

The sources of canon 1 seem to indicate that the Holy See has not, at least fundamentally, changed its former discipline in this particular matter. In the 17th century Latin missionaries who were laboring in the East proposed to the Sacred Congregation for the Propagation of the Faith the following question: "Does the Supreme Pontiff intend to include Greeks and others subject to the Sees of schismatic patriarchs in the Bull *Coena Domini* and in other Apostolic Constitutions in which he reserves cases to himself and to the Holy See?" The reply which was given to this question stated that such was not the intention of the Roman Pontiff except

45 Cappello, *De Censuris*, n. 22; Duskie, *op. cit.*, pp. 137-138; Diederichs, *The Jurisdiction of Latin Ordinaries over Their Oriental Subjects*, p. 121; Cicognani, *Canon Law*, p. 455.

46 Cf. Leo XIII, litt. ap. *Orientalium*, 30 nov. 1894, n. IX—*Fontes*, n. 627; Herman, *loc. cit.*

47 "Ubi lex non distinguit, nec nos distinguere debemus."

in the three following cases: 1) In matters of dogmas of the faith; 2) if the Holy Father in his Constitutions explicitly makes mention or disposition of them, as in the case of schismatics in the Bull *Coena Domini*; 3) if the Holy Father implicitly includes them as in the cases of appeal to future councils and of bearing arms for infidels.[48] Although this response was neither an official nor a solemn declaration of the Holy See, the majority of theologians and canonists, including Pope Benedict XIV, adhered to its general principles.[49]

The concrete and exact determination of those cases in which Orientals were implicitly included continued to offer difficulty to canonists. Pope Benedict XIV in his work, *De Ritibus*, attempted to clarify the meaning to some extent. He maintained that, although Orientals were not mentioned, they were contemplated in all those Pontifical Constitutions in which there was question of general prohibitions which for the same common reason must apply alike to Orientals and Latins.[50] The Holy See seems to have made application of the principle enunciated by Pope Benedict XIV when it explicitly declared that such was the tenor, the nature and the gravity of the Apostolic Constitutions which contained the condemnation of clandestine societies, that no one could doubt that the Roman Pontiffs had intended them to embrace all the faithful without regard to place, nation, rite or time.[51]

[48] S. C. de Prop. Fide, 4 iun. 1631—*Fontes*, n. 4449.

[49] Cf. Benedictus XIV, ep. encycl. *Allatae sunt*, 26 iul. 1755, n. 44—*Fontes*, n. 434; S. C. de Prop. Fide, litt. encycl. (ad Deleg. Ap. pro Oriente), 8 nov. 1882—*Fontes*, n. 4899.

[50] "Orientales in omnibus illis Pontificiis Constitutionibus, licet in ipsis non nominatos, comprehensos esse, in quibus Orientalibus et Occidentalibus ratio communis est. Quamobrem a Nobis etiam decretum fuit quod, licet Romanorum Pontificum Constitutiones contra Sacerdotes poenitentes ad turpia sollicitantes expressam Graecorum mentionem non faciant, non ex eo sequi ut ipsi etiam sub iisdem comprehensi non sint, quemadmodum videre est . . ." —*Benediciti XIV Papae Opera Inedita* (ed. F. Heiner, Friburgi Brisgoviae, 1904), *De Ritibus*, p. 54, as quoted in *Orientalia Christiana*, XXXII (1933), 129-130.

[51] S. C. de Prop. Fide, litt. encycl. (ad Deleg. Ap. et Ep. Orient), 24 sept. 1867—*Fontes*, n. 4871. Cf. also S. C. S. Off., decr., 21 iul. 1934—*AAS*, XXVI (1934), 550; Bouscaren, *Digest*, I, 577.

In 1882 the Sacred Congregation for the Propagation of the Faith further clarified the meaning of the implicit inclusion of Orientals under the legislation which was contained in the Apostolic Constitutions when it declared that such constitutions implicitly included Orientals whenever there was question not merely of an ecclesiastical law but of a declaration of the divine law, natural or positive. Although the Sacred Congregation admitted that this common doctrine did not have the official and authoritative sanction of the Church, it nevertheless felt justified in making application of it to impose the obligation of the *Missa pro populo* on Oriental bishops and pastors.[52]

The promulgation of the Constitution *Apostolicae Sedis*,[53] which contained the official list of papal *latae sententiae* censures, gave rise to a doubt concerning the extent to which Orientals were subject to this new penal legislation of the Holy See. The Holy Office with the approval of Pope Leo XIII answered the doubt in the following terms: 1) The Constitution *Apostolicae Sedis* has made no innovations concerning censures and their reservations for the faithful of the Oriental rites; 2) these same faithful are subject to all the censures enacted by the Holy See in matters of dogmas of the faith and in the Constitutions in which an implicit disposition is made concerning them, namely, when the subject matter shows that they are included in so far as there is question, not of a purely ecclesiastical law, but of a declaration of the natural or positive divine law.[54]

The Sacred Congregation for the Propagation of the Faith informed its apostolic delegates of this decision of the Holy Office and directed them to notify all the patriarchs, archbishops and bishops of the Oriental rites within the limits of their respective delegations of it, and of the fact that the censures and apostolic reservations enacted in the Constitution *Sacramentum poenitentiae* [55] and in the Constitutions against those who joined the Masonic sect or other similar organizations had been extended by name to Orientals.[56]

[52] Litt. encycl. (ad Deleg. Ap. pro Oriente), 8 nov. 1882—*Fontes*, n. 4899.
[53] Pius IX, 12 oct. 1869—*Fontes*, n. 552.
[54] S. C. de Prop. Fide, litt. encycl., 6 aug. 1885—*Fontes*, n. 4910.
[55] Benedictus XIV, 1 iun. 1741—*Documentum V in Codice.*
[56] S. C. de Prop. Fide, *loc. cit.*

From the time of its promulgation to the advent of the present Code this decision of the Holy Office was the authoritative norm whereby it was judged to what extent Orientals were subject to the reservations of the Holy See in which there was no express mention of Orientals. Since there is no apparent reason for thinking that the present Code has made any innovations in this particular matter, one must maintain that practically the same norm applies at the present time.[57]

There remains one point on which authors do not seem to be in agreement. Some penal laws previously contained in Apostolic Constitutions have been mitigated for the Latin Church by the law of the Code. For example, the penal law as now enacted in the Code against those who join the Masons or other similar societies [58] is not so comprehensive as was the former law.[59] Prior to the advent of the Code some of these penal laws and the reservations contained therein were explicitly extended to Orientals.[60] Are Orientals subject to the more severe penal regulations of the earlier Apostolic Constitutions, or do they benefit by the mitigations now obtaining in the Code? Some maintain that Orientals are still bound by the penal laws and reservations as enumerated in the Apostolic Constitutions which were explicitly extended to them prior to the Code.[61] Others hold that Orientals benefit in such cases by the mitigations now effected in the Code.[62]

Before accepting either of these opinions it seems necessary to

[57] Canon 6.

[58] Canon 2335.

[59] Cf. Pius IX, const. *Apostolicae Sedis*, 12 Oct. 1869, II, n. 4—*Fontes*, n. 552; Quigley, *Condemned Societies*, The Catholic University of America Canon Law Studies, n. 46 (Washington, D. C.: The Catholic University of America, 1927), pp. 73-74.

[60] Cf., e.g., Benedictus XIV, const. *Etsi pastoralis*, 26 maii 1741, § IX, n. 5—*Fontes*, n. 328; S. C. de Prop. Fide, litt. encycl. (ad Deleg. Ap. et Ep. Orient.), 24 sept. 1867—*Fontes*, n. 4871; litt. encycl., 6 aug. 1885—*Fontes*, n. 4910.

[61] Vermeersch-Creusen, *Epitome*, I, n. 68; Cicognani, *Canon Law*, pp. 456-457.

[62] Cf. Berutti, *Institutiones Iuris Canonici*, Vol. I, *Normae Generales* (Taurini-Romae: Marietti, 1936), pp. 43-44 (hereafter cited *Normae Generales*); Quigley, *loc. cit.*; Duskie, *The Canonical Status of Orientals in the United States*, pp. 130-132.

make a distinction between the different types of Apostolic Constitutions which may have been explicitly extended to Orientals. Certain Apostolic Constitutions by reason of their subject matter implicitly included Orientals. Consequently the penal laws and reservations contained therein also implicitly bound the members of the Oriental rites.[63] However, to dispel the least shadow of doubt concerning the inclusion of the Orientals, the Holy See later explicitly extended these penal regulations to the Orientals.[64]

Other Apostolic Constitutions which enacted penal laws and reservations may have pertained to purely disciplinary matters. Since the subject matter was purely disciplinary, such Constitutions or the reservations which they enacted did not even implicitly embrace Orientals. The Holy See could have extended these Constitutions to Orientals as part of their particular law. In the event that this latter type of Apostolic Constitutions and the reservations contained therein were explicitly extended to Orientals it is clear that neither the Constitution *Apostolicae Sedis* nor the Code has effected any mitigations in them, since they are related to purely disciplinary matters.[65]

Concerning the other penal laws and reservations enacted in Apostolic Constitutions which implicitly included Orientals by reason of the subject matter, both the Constitution *Apostolicae Sedis* and the Code may have effected changes for the Orientals as well as for the Latins. *Ex ipsa rei natura* all Catholics are included in such legislation. Any legislative enactment of the Holy See concerning reservations which are intimately connected with dogmas of the faith affects all Catholics.[66] Orientals should also benefit or suffer by any changes in the extent or gravity of ecclesiastical reservations enacted in Apostolic Constitutions which pertain to dogmas

[63] Cf. *supra,* pp. 78-79.

[64] E.g., Benedictus XIV, const. *Etsi pastoralis,* 26 maii 1742, § IX, n. 5—*Fontes,* n. 328; ep. encycl. *Allatae sunt,* 26 iul. 1755, n. 44—*Fontes,* n. 434; S. C. de Prop. Fide, litt. encycl. (ad Deleg. Ap. et Ep. Orient.), 24 sept. 1867—*Fontes,* n. 4871. Cf. also *supra,* p. 79.

[65] Cf. Herman, "De 'Ritu' in Iure Canonico," *Orientalia Christiana,* XXXII (1933), 125.

[66] Cf. *supra,* pp. 78-79.

of the faith or to declarations of the divine law, natural or positive.[67]

It must be remembered that both the Constitution *Apostolicae Sedis* and the Code were codifications. The former was a codification of the *latae sententiae* incurred censures enacted by the Holy See while the latter was and still remains the codification of the universal law of the Latin Church. An Apostolic Constitution was the legal instrument used in the promulgation of both these codifications.[68] Since the norm established by the Holy Office in 1885 is one of the principal sources of the first canon of the Code, its principles can be applied equally to the reservations contained in both codifications. Therefore it seems justifiable to maintain that Orientals benefit or suffer by any changes effected in the Code relative to those reservations to which Orientals were implicitly subject previously according to the principles of the Holy Office.[69]

The solution of the disputed question seems to depend on whether or not the subject matter of the Apostolic Constitutions which were later explicitly extended to Orientals pertained to dogmas of the faith or to declarations of the divine law. The reservations contained in the Apostolic Constitutions against the Masons and against those guilty of solicitation in connection with the sacrament of penance were explicitly extended to Orientals. Were these penal regulations connected purely with matters of ecclesiastical law? Did they not pertain to matters connected with Catholic doctrine or with declarations of the divine law? It is certain that the reservations enacted in these Apostolic Constitutions included Orientals for the reason that they were Catholics, and not simply in consequence of the fact that they were Orientals.[70] Hence by reason of the subject matter Orientals were implicitly comprehended in the Constitutions

[67] *Loc. cit.*

[68] Pius IX, const. *Apostolicae Sedis,* 12 oct. 1869—*Fontes,* n. 552; Benedictus XV, const. *Providentissima Mater Ecclesiae,* 27 maii 1917—*Codex Iuris Canonici,* post Card. Gasparri Praefationem in Codice.

[69] Cf. Herman, "De 'Ritu' in Iure Canonico," *Orientalia Christiana,* XXXII (1933), 124.

[70] Benedictus XIV, const. *Etsi pastoralis,* 26 maii 1742, § IX, n. 5—*Fontes,* n. 328; S. C. de Prop. Fide, litt. encycl. (ad Deleg. Ap. et Ep. Orient.), 24 sept. 1867—*Fontes,* n. 4871.

themselves; by express declaration they were also explicitly subject to the reservations enumerated therein.[71]

The Holy See is not accustomed to deal with the faithful of the Oriental rites more severely than with those of the Latin rite.[72] It seems reasonable therefore to maintain that Orientals benefit by any mitigations of the Code relative to those reservations in which they were implicitly included prior to the Code, even though these reservations also had been extended to them by means of an express declaration of the Holy See.[73]

To what reservations of the Code is the interritual penitent of the Oriental rites subject? Evidently Orientals are subject to those canons of the Latin Code which have been extended to them by means of an express declaration of the Holy See. For this reason they are subject to the *latae sententiae* contracted excommunications reserved in a most special way to the Holy See as enumerated in canons 2320, 2343, § 1, 1°, 2367 and 2369.[74] The Holy Office which is in charge of the guardianship of matters of faith and morals has declared that the reserved penal sanctions enumerated in these canons extend to the Universal Church because of the extraordinary gravity of the crimes.[75]

The Sacred Congregation for the Oriental Church has recently declared that Orientals are bound by the decrees of the Holy Office which contain the condemnation of books and papers.[76] Such decrees directly concern the doctrine of the Church rather than discipline, and have as their purpose the preservation and the protection of faith and morals.[77] This declaration of the Holy See makes it evident that Orientals, even though they are not explicitly mentioned, are bound to more than the strictly doctrinal laws of the Code. It seems that they are also included implicitly *ex ipsa rei natura* not only in those enacted reservations of the Code which

[71] S. C. de Prop. Fide, *loc. cit.*

[72] Cf. Quigley, *Condemned Societies,* p. 74.

[73] Cf. Herman, *loc. cit.*; Berutti, *Normae Generales,* pp. 43-44.

[74] S.C.S. Off., decr., 21 iul. 1934—*AAS,* XXVI (1934), 550; Bouscaren, *Digest,* II, 577-578.

[75] *Loc. cit.*

[76] Declar., 26 maii 1928—*AAS,* XX (1928), 195; Bouscaren, *Digest,* I, 685.

[77] S. C. Or., *loc. cit.*

pertain to strictly doctrinal matters, but also in those which are intimately and directly connected with the preservation and conservation of faith and morals.[78]

Such reservations extend to all the faithful, since the latter are bound not because of their membership in a particular rite but rather because of their membership in the Church as such.[79] Consequently, members of the Oriental rites, besides being subject to the reservations in the Code which have been explicitly extended to them since its promulgation, seem to be implicitly included *ex ipsa rei natura* in the reservations of sins or of censures as enumerated in canons 894, 2363,[80] 2314,[81] 2318, [82] 2319,[83] 2332 [84] and 2335.[85]

C. *The Interritual Confessor's Power to Absolve*

1. Reservations of Local Ordinaries

The primary purpose of the power of reservation is of a disciplinary character.[86] All the local bishops in the United States and

[78] Cf. Herman, "De 'Ritu' in Iure Canonico," *Orientalia Christiana,* XXXII (1933), 126-127; Duskie, *The Canonical Status of Orientals in the United States,* p. 137.

[79] Cf. *supra,* pp. 78-82.

[80] S. C. de Prop. Fide, litt. encycl., 6 aug. 1885—*Fontes,* n. 4910; *supra,* p. 78, footnote 50 and pp. 82-83.

[81] S. C. de Prop. Fide, *loc. cit.*

[82] Cf. S. C. de Prop. Fide, *loc. cit.* cum S. C. Or., declar., 26 maii 1928—*AAS,* XX (1928), 195; Bouscaren, *Digest,* I, 685; S. C. de Prop. Fide, decr., 13 apr. 1807, n. 1—*Fonti,* Serie I, Fasc. II, *Testi Vari di Diritto Nuovo* (1550-1902) (Città del Vaticano: Tipografia Poliglotta Vaticana, 1931), p. 57; Herman, "De 'Ritu' in Iure Canonico," *Orientalia Christiana,* XXXII (1933), 127.

[83] Cf. Cappello, *De Censuris,* n. 22; Duskie, *op. cit.,* pp. 136-137.

[84] Cf. S. C. de Prop. Fide, 4 iun. 1631—*Fontes,* n. 4449; Benedictus XIV ep. encycl. *Allatae sunt,* 26 iul. 1755, n. 44—*Fontes,* n. 434; *supra,* pp. 77-79.

[85] Cf. S. C. de Prop. Fide, litt. encycl. (ad Deleg. Ap. et Ep. Orient.), 23 sept. 1867—*Fontes,* n. 4871; litt. encycl., 6 aug. 1885—*Fontes,* n. 4910; Quigley, *Condemned Societies,* pp. 71-74; Augustine, *Commentary,* VIII, 343; Blat, *Commentarium Textus Codicis Iuris Canonici,* Lib. V, *De Delictis et Poenis* (1924), n. 61 (hereafter cited *De Delictis et Poenis*); *supra,* pp. 78-83.

[86] Conc. Trident., sess. XIV, *de poenitentia,* c. 7; Stadalnikas, *Reservation of Censures,* pp. 21-25; Ayrinhac, *Legislation on the Sacraments,* pp. 233-234;

Canada have the right to limit through their reservations the jurisdictional power of all confessors subject to them. Thus the jurisdiction of the confessors subject to a residential bishop of the Latin rite is limited through his reservations, while that of confessors whose jurisdiction proceeds from a Ruthenian ordinary is similarly restricted through the latter's reservations. However, no local ordinary can directly limit the jurisdiction of confessors who are not subject to him.[87]

The simultaneous existence of these canonical principles and of the distinct ritual jurisdictions in the United States and Canada could defeat the whole disciplinary purpose of the reservations of the respective local ordinaries. Any confessor whose jurisdiction is limited only through the reservations of a local ordinary of the Latin rite could absolve penitents of the Ruthenian rite from any sins reserved directly or indirectly by the latter's proper ordinary. Similarly confessors whose jurisdiction proceeds from a Ruthenian ordinary could absolve non-Ruthenian penitents from sins or censures reserved by the territorial legislation of the local Latin ordinaries.

Desirous of preserving ecclesiastical discipline and cognizant of former legislation enacted by the Holy See in similar circumstances,[88] the Sacred Congregation for the Oriental Church promulgated the following particular law for the United States and Canada:

> . . . Presbyteri vero latini absolvere non possunt fideles graeco-rutheni ritus a censuris et casibus sibi reservatis ab Ordinario graeco-rutheno absque venia eiusdem. Vicissim idem dicatur de presbyteris graeco-ruthenis quoad censuras et reservationes statutas ab Ordinario latini ritus. Ad devitandas vero difficultates, quae frequentius in praxi occurrent, Ordinarii omnes a se reservatos casus, si qui sint, sibi invicem communicent.[89]

Coronata, *De Sacramentis,* I, n. 397; Aertnys-Damen, *Theologia Moralis,* II, n. 386; Cappello, *De Poenitentia,* n. 507.

87 Canon 201, § 1.

88 E.g., S. C. de Prop. Fide (C. G.), 11 dec. 1838, ad 10, 11—*Fontes,* n. 4778; Leo XIII, litt. ap. *Orientalium,* 30 nov. 1894, n. VI—*Fontes,* n. 627.

89 Decr. *Graeci-Rutheni Ritus,* 24 maii 1930, art. 36—*AAS,* XXII (1930), 352; Bouscaren, *Digest,* I, 36-37; decr. *Cum data fuerit,* 1 mart. 1929, art. 31—*AAS,* XXI (1929), 157-158; Bouscaren, *op. cit.,* I, 14.

Since this law proceeds from that Sacred Congregation which has ample jurisdiction in interritual matters,[90] all confessors of the Latin and of the Ruthenian rites in the United States and Canada must follow its provisions.[91]

Does this prohibition of the Holy See mean that no confessor of the Greek-Ruthenian rite who has jurisdiction only from his own ordinary can absolve penitents of the Latin rite from censures and cases reserved by *any* Latin ordinary in the United States or Canada? Several reasons seem to indicate that the scope of the law is not so wide. The purpose of the law is evidently the preservation of each local ordinary's reservations. This disciplinary end would be defeated only if Greek-Ruthenian confessors could absolve Latin penitents from the territorial reservations within the very territory for which they were established. The general law of the Latin Church safeguards the applicable force of territorial reservations solely within the territory for which they were established. The Code expressly states that the reservation of a sin directly reserved (*ratione sui*) ceases outside the territory of the one reserving it,[92] while the reservation of a censure reserved in a particular territory has no binding force outside the limits of that territory.[93] Consequently outside the confines of their author's territory such reservations in no way restrict a confessor's material competence.[94]

Another indication for maintaining that this disciplinary law is not so broad in its scope is the fact that the Holy See has changed the wording of the former law on this very matter. The particular law which formerly regulated the relations between Latins and Greek-Ruthenians in the United States forbade Ruthenian confessors to absolve Latin penitents from censures and from cases reserved by the Latin *ordinaries*.[95] The present law has the singular *ordinary*

[90] Canon 257, §§ 1, 2.

[91] Cf. Dziob, *The Sacred Congregation for the Oriental Church*, The Catholic University of America Canon Law Studies, n. 214 (Washington, D. C.: The Catholic University of America Press, 1945), pp. 99-101.

[92] Canon 900, 3°.

[93] Canon 2247, § 2.

[94] Cf. Stadalnikas, *Reservation of Censures*, pp. 56-62.

[95] S. C. de Prop. Fide, decr. *Cum episcopo*, 17 aug. 1914, art. 22—*AAS*, VI (1914), 462.

instead of the plural *ordinaries.*[96] The particular law which was formerly in force in Canada contained a text which left no doubt as to the real extent of the prohibition. The text of that law explicitly stated that Ruthenian priests could not, without the permission of the Latin local ordinary, absolve penitents of the Latin rite from censures and from cases reserved in the Latin diocese in which they exercised their sacred ministry.[97]

For these reasons it seems correct to say that Greek-Ruthenian confessors in the United States and Canada are forbidden to absolve Latin penitents from simply the territorial reservations of that Latin ordinary within the confines of whose diocese the confessions are heard. Thus a Greek-Ruthenian confessor in Pittsburgh could absolve a Latin penitent who is a resident of Chicago from the sins directly or indirectly reserved in the Archdiocese of Chicago. The same confessor, however, could not absolve a Latin penitent who is a resident of Pittsburgh from the territorial reservations established by the latter's local ordinary.

Because of the vast territorial extent of the Greek-Ruthenian jurisdictions in the United States and Canada, Ruthenian penitents remain under the territorial-personal jurisdiction of their proper ordinary as long as they remain within the territorial confines of their ritual ordinariate.[98] Consequently in the United States Latin confessors who have their jurisdiction exclusively from Latin ordinaries cannot absolve the subjects of the two nationally distinct Ruthenian exarchates from sins or censures reserved by their respective Ruthenian ordinary. As long as such penitents are in the United States they remain under the territorial-personal jurisdiction of their Ruthenian ordinary. The same cannot be said of Ruthenian penitents in Canada, for the three Ruthenian exarchates there are territorially distinct.[99] Latin confessors in Canada who have their jurisdiction exclusively from Latin ordinaries can absolve Ruthenian

[96] Cf. *supra*, p. 85.

[97] S. C. de Prop. Fide, decr. *Fidelibus Ruthenis*, 18 aug. 1913, art. 28: ". . . Presbyteri vero rutheni absolvere non poterunt fideles latini ritus a censuris et a casibus reservatis in dioecesi latina in qua sacrum ministerium exercent, absque venia Ordinarii latini . . ."—*AAS*, V (1913), 397.

[98] Cf. *supra*, pp. 12-15.

[99] Cf. *supra*, p. 14.

penitents from the personal-territorial reservations established by Ruthenian ordinaries provided such penitents are beyond the territorial boundaries of their own exarchate.[100]

To avoid practical difficulties the Holy See has directed the local ordinaries of both the Latin and the Greek-Ruthenian rites in North America to notify one another of the reservations they have made.[101] In the United States this means that the local ordinaries of the Latin rite must notify the two Ruthenian apostolic exarchs of their reservations, while each of the latter must send a similar notification to each of the local ordinaries of the Latin rite. In Canada the local ordinaries of the Latin rite whose dioceses are situated within the territorial confines of one of the Ruthenian exarchates must notify the Ruthenian exarch of their reservations, while the Ruthenian apostolic exarchs must similarly notify each of the Latin ordinaries who have territorial jurisdiction within their exarchate. Evidently the transmission of these notifications entails more work for the Ruthenian chancery offices than for the Latin ones.[102]

The interritual confessor must also realize that within the territorial limits of his jurisdiction he cannot absolve any penitent, even though he belong to another ritual or territorial jurisdiction, from sins directly reserved (*ratione sui*) by his own local ordinary.[103] However, if the sin is only indirectly reserved by the local ordinary in view of an attached censure, and if the interritual penitent has not incurred the censure, the same principle does not hold. In such a case the sin is not reserved for the simple reason that the censure has not been incurred.[104]

Relative to the reservations established by ordinaries, interritual

[100] Cf. *infra*, pp. 69-70.

[101] Cf. *supra*, p. 85.

[102] Cf. "Diocesan Censures *Latae Sententiae* and Reserved Sins in the United States," *Theological Studies* (Woodstock, Md., 1940—), VIII (1947), 365-405. This article contains lists of the reserved sins and of the reserved *latae sententiae* censures established by the local ordinaries of the United States. Therein interritual confessors of the Ruthenian rite will find lists for the various Latin dioceses while confessors of the Latin rite will find similar information concerning the Ruthenian jurisdictions.

[103] P. C. I., 24 nov. 1920—*AAS*, XII (1920), 575; Bouscaren, *Digest*, I, 415.

[104] Canon 2246, § 3.

confessors must be mindful of the legislation of canon 900. This canon enumerates the various circumstances in the presence of which all reservations of sin (*ratione sui*) cease to have any juridic effect on the jurisdiction of the confessor.[105] The Pontifical Commission for the Interpretation of the Code has declared that the legislation contained in this canon refers only to sins reserved directly or *ratione sui*.[106] It is certain that any confessor irrespective of rite can take advantage of these provisions to absolve penitents from the one sin directly reserved by the Holy See [107] and from sins reserved by the ordinaries of the Latin rite. Concerning sins reserved by Oriental ordinaries there are divergent opinions. Herman maintains that the favors of canon 900 cannot be applied to sins directly reserved by Oriental ordinaries, since the prescriptions of the law are prejudicial to the latter's jurisdiction.[108] He would require an explicit declaration of the Holy See before extending the favors of the law to the sins directly reserved by Oriental ordinaries.[109] Cappello on the contrary holds that the milder discipline of the Code must be applied to Orientals also, since the purpose of the law is the spiritual good of souls.[110] He seems to base his opinion on the Instruction of the Holy Office which was one of the principal sources of canon 900.[111] According to Cappello the norms established by the Holy Office in this Instruction of 1916 applied to Orientals as

105 Canon 900.—Quaevis reservatio omni vi caret:

1°. Cum confessionem peragunt sive aegroti qui domo egredi non valent, sive sponsi matrimonii ineundi causa;

2°. Quoties vel legitimus Superior petitam pro aliquo determinato casu absolvendi facultatem denegaverit, vel prudenti confessarii iudicio absolvendi facultas a legitimo Superiore peti nequeat sine gravi poenitentis incommodo aut sine periculo violationis sigilli sacramentalis;

3°. Extra territorium reservantis, etiamsi dumtaxat ad absolutionem obtinendam poenitens ex eo discesserit.

106 10 nov. 1925, ad I—*AAS*, XVII (1925), 583; Bouscaren, *Digest*, I, 415.

107 P. C. I., 10 nov. 1925, ad II—*AAS*, XVII (1925), 583; Bouscaren, *op. cit.*, I, 416.

108 "De 'Ritu' in Iure Canonico," *Orientalia Christiana*, XXXII (1933), 136-137.

109 Herman, *loc. cit.*

110 *De Poenitentia*, n. 1048.

111 S.C.S. Off., instr., 13 iul. 1916—*AAS*, VIII (1916), 313-315.

well as to Latins.[112] Until the matter is definitely settled the interritual confessor can follow the milder opinion and make use of canon 900 to absolve penitents from sins reserved directly by Oriental ordinaries.[113]

2. Reservations of the Holy See

The reservations established by the Holy See for members of the Latin rite in general are contained in the Code. Members of the Oriental rites are also subject to some of these reservations.[114] The one sin directly reserved to the Holy See and the reserved censures which include Orientals as well as Latins need offer no special problem to the interritual confessor. All the members of the Church, irrespective of rite, are subject to such reservations and their juridic effects. Consequently no confessor without faculties from the Holy See can *ordinarily* absolve a penitent guilty of the false denunciation of an innocent priest before an ecclesiastical tribunal relative to the matter of solicitation in connection with the sacrament of penance.[115] No confessor is ordinarily empowered to absolve any penitent from those censures to which all members of the Church are subject or from the sins which may be thereby indirectly reserved unless he has been granted the power by law or by delegation.[116]

What is to be held regarding those censures which are reserved in the purely disciplinary canons of the Code? Orientals are not subject to such laws, and hence they likewise are not subject to the penalties which are reserved therein.[117] Penitents of the Oriental rites who commit sins which the purely disciplinary canons of the Code reserve by reason of the attached censure would not incur the censure for they are not subject to these penal laws. Therefore any

[112] *De Poenitentia,* n. 1045, 2.

[113] Cf. canons 15 and 209.

[114] Cf. *supra,* pp. 76-84.

[115] Cf. canon 894; Cappello, *De Poenitentia,* n. 1033; *supra,* pp. 78-84.

[116] Cf. canons 2236; 2253; 2246, § 3, and 2250, §§ 1-2.

[117] Cf. *supra,* pp. 76-84; Kelly, *The Jurisdiction of the Confessor,* pp. 72-73; Duskie, *The Canonical Status of Orientals in the United States,* pp. 137-139.

interritual confessor could absolve Oriental penitents from such sins precisely for the reason that they are not reserved.[118]

If a penitent of the Latin rite were guilty of a delict through his violation of one of the purely disciplinary penal canons of the Code he would incure the penalty. For example, if a religious of the Latin rite became an apostate from his religious institute, he would automatically incur an excommunication which is reserved to his major superior or, in the event that the institute is of a lay character or without the prerogative of exemption, to the local ordinary.[119] Could an interritual confessor of an Oriental rite absolve such a penitent from the censure and from the sin which is indirectly reserved because of the attached censure? Some authors have expressed the opinion that Greek-Ruthenian confessors in the United States and Canada could absolve Latin penitents from any censure reserved by the Code except those to which all Orientals are subject.[120] The basic reason for this opinion is that these Oriental confessors are not subject to the Code and therefore their jurisdiction is not restricted except by those reservations which *natura rei* or *nominatim* apply to Orientals. It has been maintained that this opinion has at least a probability of correctness on its side.[121]

It must be admitted that the Latin Code is a law of capacity which was primarily codified for members of the Latin Church.[122] Members of the Oriental rites are subject to its laws only in so far as they are included by reason of canon 1. Although the faithful of the Oriental rites are not subject to the purely disciplinary penal canons of the Code,[123] nevertheless Oriental confessors in exercising jurisdiction in the internal sacramental forum may well be subject to the general principles of the Holy See as established in the Code pertinent to the absolution of reserved censures.

The primary purpose of reservation is to bring the more serious

118 Canon 2246, § 3.

119 Canon 2385.

120 Kelly, *op. cit.*, pp. 77-78; Duskie, *op. cit.*, p. 141.

121 Kelly, *loc. cit.*; Duskie, *loc. cit.*

122 Cf. Plöchl, "The Fundamental Principles of the Philosophy of Canon Law," *The Jurist*, IV (1944), 75-76.

123 Cf. *supra*, p. 90.

crimes to the judgment of higher ecclesiastical superiors.[124] The direct object of the reservation of a censure is the ecclesiastical penalty, the censure itself.[125] The act of the competent ecclesiastical superior who reserves such a penalty to himself or to other determined persons implies that the necessary power to absolve from the reserved censure is denied to others who are subject to his jurisdiction.[126] The Roman Pontiff is the author of the reserved censures which are enacted in the Latin Code. The jurisdiction of all inferiors in the external as well as in the internal forum is subject to his supreme jurisdiction.[127]

When the supreme legislator reserves certain censures to the Holy See or to other specified ecclesiastics it is certainly his intention that both the purpose and the direct object of his legislative acts be encompassed by his law.[128] The achievement of these two aims demands *ex ipsa rei natura* that the material competence of all inferior confessors be restricted once a censure which is reserved through the general legislation of the Roman Pontiff has been contracted. Therefore the nature of the subject matter, the purpose and the direct object of the reservation of censures demand that certain juridic principles of the Holy See relative to the absolution of reserved censures extend to all inferior confessors irrespective of rite.

These general principles of papal law are contained in the Code. According to canon 2253, outside the danger of death only the following can absolve: a) From a censure inflicted *ab homine*, he to whom it is reserved, namely, the one who inflicted the censure, his competent superior, his successor, or his delegate; [129] b) from a censure reserved *a iure*, he who established it or he to whom it is reserved, and their successors, competent superiors or delegates.

124 Conc. Trident., sess. XIV, *de poenitentia*, c. 7; Stadalnikas, *Reservation of Censures*, p. 26.

125 Cf. *supra*, pp. 71-72.

126 Cf. *supra*, pp. 72-73.

127 Cf. *supra*, pp. 5-6, 71.

128 ". . . melius putamus reservationem delinquentes nonnisi mediate seu indirecte afficere, directe vero et immediate vel ipsas censuras in se spectatas vel eos quibus a censuris absolvere generatim ius est . . ." Coronata, *Institutiones*, IV, n. 1749. Cf. also Stadalnikas, *Reservation of Censures*, n. 24.

129 Canons 2253, 2°, and 2245, § 2.

Hence from a censure reserved to a bishop or an ordinary, any ordinary can absolve his subjects, and the local ordinary can absolve even travelers (*peregrini*); from a censure reserved to the Holy See the power, general if simply reserved, special if it is specially reserved, and finally most special if it is most specially reserved, without prejudice to the provisions of canon 2254.[130] Cappello's opinion that these general principles of papal law extend to Orientals as well as to Latins seems to be in accord with the intention of the legislator and with the purpose and nature of the reservation of censures.[131]

The Roman Pontiffs and the Sacred Congregations, always solicitous about the preservation of the proper discipline in the Church, for centuries have enacted particular legislation which had as its purpose the protection of the reservations established by the local ordinaries of the Oriental as well as of the Latin rite.[132] The exercise of this solicitude in the safeguarding of the reservations of intermediate legislators indicates that the supreme legislator desires his own reservations both to fulfill their primary purpose and to reach their direct object. Finally, the particular law of various Oriental rites explicitly forbids inferior confessors to absolve from cases reserved to higher ecclesiastical superiors.[133]

[130] Canon 2253, 3°.

[131] *Summa Iuris Canonici,* I, n. 62.

[132] Cf., e. g., Benedictus XIV, ep. encycl. *Demandatam,* 24 dec. 1743, § 12—*Fontes,* n. 338; Leo XIII, litt. ap. *Orientalium,* 30 nov. 1894, n. VI—*Fontes,* n. 627; S. C. de Prop. Fide (C. G.), 17 febr. 1772, ad 3—*Fontes,* n. 4555; decr. *Cum Episcopo,* 17 aug. 1914, art. 22—*AAS,* VI (1914), 462; decr. *Fidelibus Ruthenis,* 18 aug. 1913, art. 28—*AAS,* V (1913), 397; S. C. Or., decr. *Cum data fuerit,* 1 mart. 1929, art. 31—*AAS,* XXI (1929), 157-158; decr. *Graeci-Rutheni Ritus,* 24 maii 1930, art. 36—*AAS,* XXII (1930), 353.

[133] E. g., Synodus Provincialis Ruthenorum (1720), sess. III, tit. 3: ". . . Confessarii vero casus omnes Summo Pontifici, et Episcopis reservatos, scriptos apud se habeant; ne quid per incuriam sibi facultatem assumant."—*Synodus Provincialis Zamostena,* p. 77.

Concilium Nationis Armenorum (1911), tit. III, cap. 6: "Declaramus igitur et agnoscimus reservandi facultatem primum ac praecipue in Romano Pontifice pro suprema, qua pollet in universa Ecclesia potestate; deinceps etiam in Reverendissimo D. Patriarcha pro potestate ipsi in Armenos catholicos a R. Pontifice tradita . . . ut quisque intelligere valeat . . . ab his quae suo iudicio Patriarcha et Summus Pontifex reservare voluerint, neminem sive in

For these reasons it seems correct to maintain that the material competence of Oriental confessors is sometimes *ex ipsa rei natura* limited in consequence of certainly incurred censures which have been reserved through the law of the Code to higher superiors.[134] It is true that Oriental confessors, just as other members of the Oriental rites, are not directly subject to any of the purely disciplinary penal canons of the Code, in the sense namely that they do not incur the penalties enacted in these canons precisely for the reason that these canons are not legislated for them. Any confessor could absolve any penitent of the Oriental rites though the latter's action materially contravened the penal legislation contained in the canons, for such a penitent has not thereby incurred any reserved censure. On the other hand, if a penitent of the Latin rite has incurred a censure which by the supreme lawgiver has been reserved for its absolution to the higher ecclesiastical superiors in the Church, then the jurisdiction of the interritual confessor of the Oriental rite is also automatically restricted, for this object does not fall within his material competence. Jurisdiction over that material object has been denied to all confessors of lower rank and status by the highest authority in the Church, the Roman Pontiff. The opinon therefore which maintains that Greek-Ruthenian confessors in the United States and Canada can absolve any Latin penitent from any censure reserved in the Code except those to which Orientals are subject does not seem tenable.[135] It seems not to furnish any sufficient basis for any intrinsic probability of correctness.

It is certain that all Oriental confessors who have received a delegated jurisdiction from Latin ordinaries cannot ordinarily absolve from the reservations enacted in the Latin Code. The jurisdiction of these confessors is delegated. It is therefore necessarily a participation of the jurisdiction possessed by the Latin ordinaries. The latter's ordinary jurisdiction does not extend beyond the cases re-

patriarchatu sive in tota Ecclesia posse absolvere, nisi absolvendi facultatem a Patriarcha vel a Summo Pontifice impetraverit. . . . Sciant ergo confessarii, se absolvere non posse absque facultate a casibus et censuris Sedi Apostolicae vel loci Ordinario reservatis."—*Acta et Decreta Nationis Armenorum Romae habiti ad Sancti Nicolai Tolentinatis anno MDCCCCXI*, nn. 479-480.

[134] Canon 18.

[135] Cf. *supra*, p. 91.

served to them by the Code itself and to occult cases simply reserved to the Holy See.[136] Although Latin ordinaries may grant to confessors of the Oriental rites a participation of their own power,[137] they evidently cannot make concessions of powers which they themselves do not possess. Hence these Oriental confessors cannot go beyond the limits of their delegated power in absolving penitents of the Latin rite from sins or censures reserved by the Latin Code.[138]

Article 2. Extension of Material Competence

The preceding article makes it clear that the confessor's power to absolve from sins and censures is limited as a result of the reservations of his lawful ecclesiastical superiors. It is clear, too, that the confessor as such ordinarily does not possess the power to dispense penitents from matrimonial impediments,[139] from irregularities,[140] and from vindictive penalties.[141] Nor is the confessor ordinarily empowered to commute the works which are prescribed for gaining of indulgences.[142]

Although the Church sanctions such restrictions of the confessor's material competence, it at the same time keeps in view the salvation of souls. As a consequence ecclesiastical law envisages special conditions and circumstances in the presence of which an extension of the confessor's material competence is necessary or at least

136 Canons 2253, 3°, and 2237, § 2.

137 Canon 199, § 1.

138 Canon 203, § 1.

139 Canons 80 and 1040.

140 Canons 80 and 983. Cf. also Hickey, *Irregularities and Simple Impediments in the New Code of Canon Law,* The Catholic University of America Canon Law Studies, n. 7 (Washington, D. C.: The Catholic University of America, 1920), pp. 86-88.

141 Canons 2236, § 1, and 2289-2290. Cf. also Christ, *Dispensation from Vindicative Penalties,* The Catholic University of America Canon Law Studies, n. 174 (Washington, D. C.: The Catholic University of America Press, 1943), pp. 70-71; 168-171.

142 Canon 935; S. C. Indulg., *Lausanen. et Geneven.,* 16 ian. 1886, ad I, III—*Fontes,* n. 5093; *Urbis et Orbis,* 18 sept. 1862—*Fontes,* n. 5065. Cf. also Hagedorn, *General Legislation on Indulgences,* The Catholic University of America Canon Law Studies, n. 22 (Washington, D. C.: The Catholic University of America, 1924), pp. 105-109.

useful for the greater good of souls. Thus it is that the law of the Church, under specified conditions and often with limitations, gives the confessor the following extensive powers:

1. To absolve from reserved sins and censures; [143]

2. To dispense from certain matrimonial impediments and from the prescribed form of marriage; [144]

3. To dispense in the more urgent occult cases from irregularities which arise from occult delicts, in order to enable the penitent to exercise lawfully the orders he has already received; [145]

4. To grant a suspension of or even a dispensation from *latae sententiae* vindictive penalties in the more urgent occult cases; [146]

5. To commute the works which are prescribed for the gaining of indulgences.[147]

When the conditions or circumstances postulated by the law in each case are fulfilled, all confessors of the Latin rite automatically possess the extensive powers which are granted by the law of the Latin Church. It is certain that these same confessors may make use of these ample powers in favor of any penitent of the Latin rite who at the moment falls within the field of their local or personal competence. Do confessors of the Oriental rites also enjoy the same extensive powers? May confessors make use of their broad powers in favor of penitents who belong to a rite other than their own? Apparently these particular problems have never been explicitly or

[143] Canons 882, 2252 and 2254. Cf. also Coronata, *Institutiones,* IV, nn. 1760-1764; *De Sacramentis,* I, n. 359; Ayrinhac, *Penal Legislation,* nn. 95-106; Beste, *Introductio,* pp. 909-914; Augustine, *Commentary,* VIII, 151-162; Moriarity, *The Extraordinary Absolution from Censures,* The Catholic University of America Canon Law Studies, n. 113 (Washington, D. C.: The Catholic University of America, 1938), pp. 69-290; Kelly, *The Jurisdiction of the Confessor,* pp. 90-99.

[144] Canons 1044 and 1045, § 3. Cf. also Coronata, *De Sacramentis,* III, nn. 159-160; Vermeersch-Creusen, *Epitome,* II, n. 312; Augustine, *op. cit.,* V, 96-109; Kelly, *op. cit.,* pp. 99-116; 213-231.

[145] Canon 990, § 2.

[146] Canon 2290. Cf. also Christ, *op. cit.,* pp. 169-247.

[147] Canon 935. Cf. also Hagedorn, *General Legislation on Indulgences,* pp. 108-109.

authentically resolved by the Holy See. They may however prove to be real practical difficulties for interritual confessors, especially in the United States and Canada.

Some authors have expressed the view that Orientals benefit by all the favors enumerated in the Latin Code.[148] This view does not seem to be correct, for the Holy See on different occasions has expressly declared that priests of the Oriental rites may not take advantage of the privilege of saying three Masses on All Souls' Day.[149] On the other hand, it would also be incorrect to maintain that Orientals are not the beneficiaries of any of the favorable concessions which are mentioned in the Latin Code. The Sacred Penitentiary, for example, has authoritatively decreed that the faithful of the Oriental rites can gain all the general indulgences granted by the Holy Father.[150] Consequently, either a positive or a negative general statement concerning the participation of Orientals in the favorable concessions enumerated in the Latin Code would be equally unwarranted. It must be remembered that the Latin Code effects no change in the discipline of the Oriental Church unless such a change is evident from an express provision of law or from the very nature of the case (*ex ipsa rei natura*).[151] To arrive at a suitable and justifiable solution for this particular problem, consideration must therefore be given to the nature of the particular favors and to their relation to the existing discipline of the Oriental Church.[152]

Canons 882, 935, 990, § 2, 1044, 1045, § 3, 2252, 2254 and 2290 certainly reflect favorable laws. They give powers to confessors which may be called faculties or privileges in a wide sense.[153] As is evident from their text, these favorable concessions are given to confessors for use only in the internal forum. Once the essential

[148] E. g., Maroto, *Institutiones Iuris Canonici* (2 vols., Vol. I, 3. ed., Romae, 1921), I, n. 173; De Meester, *Juris Canonici et Juris Canonico-Civilis Compendium* (nova ed., 3 vols. in 4, Brugis, 1921-1928), I, n. 112.

[149] S. C. de Prop. Fide, 13 mart. 1916, ad I et II—*AAS,* VIII (1916), 104-105; S. C. Or., 19 dec. 1928, ad 5—Bouscaren, *Digest,* I, 5. Cf. also Michiels, *Normae Generales,* I, 46.

[150] 7 iul. 1917—*AAS,* IX (1917), 399; Bouscaren, *op. cit.,* I, 42.

[151] Canon 1.

[152] Michiels, *loc. cit.*; Cicognani, *Canon Law,* pp. 459-460.

[153] Cicognani, *op. cit.,* pp. 782-783; 850-853; Herman, "De 'Ritu' in Iure Canonico," *Orientalia Christiana,* XXXII (1933), 136.

conditions as postulated in each case are fulfilled, the Church extends the material competence of the confessor in view of souls who find themselves in a state of spiritual need or emergency.[154] Now, the primary purpose of the jurisdictional power which is exercised in the internal forum is to direct and to judge an individual's moral actions in their relation to God for the private and immediate benefit of the individual.[155] Consequently the favorable concessions, minutely described in the canons enumerated above, have as their primary and proximate end the good of souls.[156] Such favorable concessions seem to be spiritual in nature, and do not seem to militate against the present discipline of the Oriental Church.[157]

Furthermore, it seems only proper to assume that the supreme legislator intends and desires all members of the Church, irrespective of their rite, to be the recipients and the beneficiaries of the same consideration and liberality, especially when there is question of concessions or favors which have as their primary and proximate end the good of individual souls.[158] Pope Pius XII has only recently given an indication of this intention. He has placed his stamp of approval on the recently promulgated Law on the Sacrament of Matrimony for the Oriental Church. This new legislation explicitly gives to confessors of the Oriental rites powers to dispense from matrimonial impediments and from the prescribed form of

[154] Cf. S. R. R., *Nullitatis Matrimonii,* 25 maii 1925, Coram R. P. D. Ubaldo Mannucci, Decisio XXV, n. 3—*Sacrae Romanae Rotae Sententiae seu Decisiones* ab anno 1909 (Typis Polyglottis Vaticanis, 1912—), XVII (1925), 198. In this case the Rota discussed the power of a Latin ordinary to dispense a traveller (*peregrinus*) from matrimonial impediments, and with reference to the intention of the legislator declared the following. ". . . legislator voluit Episcopos vi Codicis tanta munitos esse potestate, ut, *quoties utilitas Ecclesiae et animarum salus id requirat,* communis legis rigorem temperare et iustas dispensationes largiri aeque opportuneque valeant."

[155] Cf. *supra,* pp. 2-3.

[156] Cf. Herman, *loc. cit.*; Cappello, *De Poenitentia,* n. 594, 1; *Tractatus Canonico-Moralis de Sacramentis* (3 vols., Vol. III, *De Matrimonio,* 2. ed. Taurinorum Augustae: Marietti, 1927), n. 923 (hereafter cited *De Matrimonio*); Duskie, *The Canonical Status of Orientals in the United States,* p. 178.

[157] Cf. Herman, *loc. cit.*

[158] Herman, "De 'Ritu' in Iure Canonico," *Orientalia Christiana,* XXXII (1933), 136.

marriage similar to those expressly granted to Latin confessors by the Latin Code.[159]

The complete Code of Law for the Oriental Church will most probably contain other provisions which explicitly extend the material competence of confessors of the Oriental rites in view of penitents who find themselves in a state of spiritual need or emergency. Such extensions in all probability will be similar to those described in the canons under discussion here. However, until the complete Oriental Code is promulgated, there seems sufficient reason to maintain that confessors of the Oriental rites may make use of the extensions of material competence according to the conditions described in canons 882, 935, 990, § 2, 2252, 2254 and 2290.[160]

There seems to be no one who denies that confessors of the Oriental rites may make use of the powers listed in canons 882, 935, 2252 and 2254.[161] Prior to the recent promulgation of the Oriental Law on Marriage some authors held that Orientals did not participate in the benefits outlined in canons 1043-1045.[162] Since May 2, 1949, when this new legislation went into effect, there can be no doubt that confessors of the Oriental rites possess the same dispensatory power as do confessors of the Latin rite relative to matrimonial impediments and the prescribed form of marriage.[163]

It must be admitted that some authors still do not admit that Oriental confessors have the right to make use of the extensions of material competence listed in canons 990, § 2, and 2290. For example, Rodrigo and Christ maintain that these favorable conces-

[159] Pius XII, motu propr. *Crebrae allatae,* 22 febr. 1949, can. 33-35—*AAS,* XXXXI (1949), 96-97. Compare these canons with canons 1043-1045 of the Latin Code.

[160] Cf. Cappello, *De Poenitentia,* nn. 594, 1, 1045 and 1048; *De Matrimonio,* n. 923; *Summa Iuris Canonici,* I, n. 62; *De Censuris,* n. 132; Herman, *loc. cit.*; Moriarity, *Extraordinary Absolution from Censures,* pp. 77, 155 and 157; Duskie, *loc. cit.*

[161] Cf. Cappello, *loc. cit.*; Moriarity, *loc. cit.*; Herman, *loc. cit.*; Diederichs, *The Jurisdiction of Latin Ordinaries over Their Oriental Subjects,* pp. 51, 115-116; Rodrigo, *Praelectiones Theologico-Moralis Comillenis,* Series I, *Theologia Moralis Fundamentalis,* Tom. II, *Tractatus de Legibus* (Santander: Sal Terrae, 1944), p. 439, n. 601, c (hereafter cited *De Legibus*).

[162] Cf. e. g., Rodrigo, *loc. cit.*

[163] Cf. *supra,* p. 98.

sions do not *ex ipsa rei natura* apply to Orientals.[164] Christ argues that, since vindictive penalties are pure penalties and do not prevent the reception of the sacraments, the faculties granted to confessors in canon 2290 cannot be used by confessors other than those of the Latin rite.[165]

One must agree that vindictive penalties do not prevent a person from receiving the sacraments and that an irregularity is a perpetual impediment which prohibits only the lawful reception and exercise of the power of Orders.[166] However, the extraordinary powers delineated in canons 990, § 2, and 2290 are given to the confessor not merely that he may enable the penitent to receive the sacraments. In both these extraordinary extensions of the confessor's material competence the supreme legislator seems to have in view the spiritual good of a penitent in need of such extraordinary dispensatory power in order to be freed from the obligation of observing the vindictive penalty or irregularity, and of revealing his secret sin which would entail grave harm, loss of reputation, or scandal.[167] Christ himself seems to admit this, for in describing the nature of an *occult more urgent case* as postulated in canon 2290 he states: "The occult case is established by the fact that the delict is at least formally occult or the penalty is occult; and the more urgent case is established by the fact that as a result of the observance of the penalty incurred the delinquent would make known his secret sin, which would entail loss of reputation or scandal."[168] Consequently, the very nature and purpose of these favorable concessions seem to justify the opinion which holds that confessors of the Oriental rites may also make use of them.[169]

164 Rodrigo, *De Legibus, loc. cit.*; Christ, *Dispensation from Vindicative Penalties*, p. 188.

165 *Dispensation from Vindicative Penalties, loc. cit.*

166 Vermeersch-Creusen, *Epitome*, II, n. 252.

167 Cf. Berutti, *Institutiones Iuris Canonici*, Vol. VI, *De Delictis et Poenis* (Taurini-Romae: Marietti, 1938), n. 86, II; Ayrinhac, *Penal Legislation*, n. 157; Vermeersch-Creusen, *Epitome*, III, n. 471; Kelly, *The Jurisdiction of the Confessor*, pp. 233-234.

168 *Dispensation from Vindicative Penalties*, p. 171.

169 Cf. Herman, "De 'Ritu' in Iure Canonico," *Orientalia Christiana*, XXXII (1933), 136.

May confessors make use of these extensions of their material competence in favor of penitents who belong to a rite other than their own? The laws in which these ample faculties are enumerated do not restrict their use to the members of one's own rite.[170] In the internal sacramental forum the title of subjection to the confessor's power to dispense as well as to his power to absolve is the penitential character of the person over whom the power is exercised.[171] Provided the penitent is otherwise subject to their personal or local jurisdiction, there seems to be no justifiable reason for restricting Latin or Oriental confessors to members of their own rite in the exercise of the extraordinary power to absolve and to dispense which they possess in virtue of the common law of the Church. Consequently, confessors of the Latin rite may make use of their extraordinary material competence in favor of penitents of the Oriental rites, and confessors of the Oriental rites may do likewise in favor of penitents of the Latin rite.[172]

Christ would not agree with this conclusion, for he excludes confessors and penitents from the use of the benefits delineated in canon 2290. He says: "Since canon 2290 seems to be restricted to members of the Latin rite, the penitent must be of the Latin rite. Orientals, it seems, are to be excluded from the benefits of this canon. Apparently, therefore, an Oriental penitent cannot be validly and licitly granted a suspension of or a dispensation from a vindicative penalty by a Latin confessor."[173]

This statement does not seem to be consistent with what the same author has maintained elsewhere in his work. When this author discussed the subject of the dispensatory power which local ordinaries possess in virtue of canon 2237, he said: *"If the dispensatory power of canon 2237 is exercised in the internal sacramental forum, the jurisdictional relationship is verified by the penitential*

[170] Cf. canons 882; 935; 900, § 2; 1044; 1045, § 3; 2252; 2254 and 2290.

[171] Michiels, *Normae Generales*, II, n. 492.

[172] Cf. Cappello, *De Poenitentia*, n. 594, 1; 1038-1039; 1045 and 1048; *De Matrimonio*, n. 923; Duskie, *The Canonical Status of Orientals in the United States*, pp. 177-178; Moriarity, *Extraordinary Absolution from Censures*, pp. 77, 155 and 157; Herman, *loc. cit.*; Marbach, *Marriage Legislation for the Catholics of the Oriental Rites in the United States and Canada*, pp. 224-225.

[173] Christ, *Dispensation from Vindicative Penalties*, p. 188.

character of the one who presents himself to the competent superior. Consequently, if a local ordinary is approached in the confessional, his jurisdiction extends over all those over whom he has sacramental jurisdiction according to canon 881, § 1, and is not limited as it is in the external forum."[174]

Canon 881, § 1, refers to the personal competence of the confessors who possess local jurisdiction of the internal sacramental forum. It states that *all* confessors with local jurisdiction have the right to absolve validly and lawfully any penitent who approaches their local tribunal, even penitents of the Oriental rites. The canon does not state that only those confessors who are local ordinaries have this right. The text of the law is quite general and includes all local confessors of which local ordinaries are only a particular group. Therefore, Christ, who admits that local ordinaries of the Latin rite in the internal sacramental forum may use the dispensatory power, as granted in canon 2237, in favor of penitents of the Oriental rites who approach their local tribunal, should at least logically admit that local confessors of the Latin rite may similarly use the dispensatory power, as granted in canon 2290, in favor of penitents of the Oriental rites.

[174] Christ, *op. cit.*, pp. 129-130 (Italics not in the original text).

CONCLUSIONS

1. The legislation of the IV Lateran Council (1215) all but excluded the possibility of the interritual administration of the sacrament of penance. However, the papal confessional privileges which religious Orders acquired shortly after this council soon neutralized the restrictive effect of its legislation on the interritual administration of the sacrament of penance (pp. 17-25).

2. After the Council of Trent numerous decrees and instructions of the Holy See give evidence of the Church's practice of not restricting the administration of the sacrament of penance on the basis of ritual diversity between confessor and penitent. Consequently, canons 881, § 1 and 905 cannot be said to contain new legislation. They are rather the universal expressions of the legitimacy of a practice commonly accepted in the Church for centuries, namely, the approved interritual administration of the sacrament of penance (pp. 25-28).

3. No one, except the Bishop of Rome, could enact legislation contrary to the interritual right of penitents. Neither an ordinary nor a pastor could lawfully forbid his subjects to confess their sins to confessors of another rite who are otherwise competent. Neither could ordinaries, simply on the score of diversity of rite, lawfully prevent competent confessors from absolving penitents who belonged to a different rite. With the possible exception of confessors of the Italo-Greek rite, no duly authorized confessor can lawfully refuse simply on the basis of a ritual diversity to hear the confession of a penitent (pp. 31-34).

4. It is maintained that, irrespective of their rite, all confessors who possess local jurisdiction enjoy the same extensive personal competence, as described in canon 881, § 1, within the local extent of their jurisdictional power (pp. 35-37).

5. The interritual confessor with local jurisdiction absolves travellers (*peregrini*) in virtue either of his ordinary local jurisdiction or of the delegated local jurisdiction which he has received from the ordinary of the place where the confessions are heard (pp. 37-40).

6. In the United States and Canada confessors who have received their local jurisdiction solely from a Latin ordinary cannot in virtue of that jurisdiction lawfully and validly act as local confessors in Ruthenian churches or oratories. Similarly, confessors who have received jurisdiction solely from a Ruthenian ordinary would exceed the limits of their local competence were they in virtue of such granted jurisdiction to act as local confessors in churches or oratories under the exclusive jurisdiction of a Latin ordinary. Their action would be not only unlawful but also invalid (pp. 40-42).

7. The interritual confessor with ordinary personal jurisdiction can validly hear the confessions of his subjects anywhere, even in churches and oratories which are under the exclusive jurisdiction of an ordinary of a canonically different rite. In the absence of any contrary law pastors who belong to the Oriental rites seem to be justified in making practical application of this norm (pp. 55-59).

8. The common law of the Church gives cardinals, bishops and women religious, in certain cases, the right to choose priests to hear their confessions. Their use of this option indirectly causes the priests so chosen to obtain the necessary personal jurisdiction to absolve them. Ecclesiastical law does not restrict cardinals, bishops or women religious in the use of their privileges to priests of their own rite. They have the right to select as their confessors priests who belong to a rite other than their own (pp. 63-69).

9. Orientals seem to be subject, not only to those reservations of the Latin Code which have been explicitly extended to them since the promulgation of this body of laws, but also *ex ipsa rei natura,* to the reservations of sins or censures which are described in canons 894, 2314, 2318, 2319, 2332, 2335 and 2363 (pp. 76-84).

10. In consequence of particular legislation enacted by the Holy See for the United States and Canada interritual confessors of the Latin rite are forbidden to absolve penitents of the Ruthenian rite from incurred censures and cases reserved by a Ruthenian ordinary as long as such penitents are within the territorial boundaries of their exarchate. They may only do so with the authorization of the Ruthenian ordinary concerned. Interritual confessors of the Ruthenian rite are likewise forbidden to absolve penitents of the Latin rite from incurred censures and cases reserved by the ordinary

of the Latin diocese within the local boundaries of which the confessions are heard (pp. 84-88).

11. The interritual confessor can certainly make use of canon 900 in absolving from sins directly reserved (*ratione sui*) by the Holy See and Latin ordinaries, and in all probability even from sins so reserved by Oriental ordinaries (pp. 88-90).

12. It is maintained that the material competence of Oriental confessors is sometimes *ex ipsa rei natura* limited in consequence of certainly incurred censures which have been reserved through the law of the Latin Code to higher superiors. Thus, if a penitent of the Latin rite has incurred a censure which by the supreme legislator has been reserved for its absolution to the higher ecclesiastical superiors in the Church, the jurisdiction of the interritual confessor of an Oriental rite is automatically restricted, for this object does not fall within his material competence. Jurisdiction over that material object has been denied to all confessors of lower rank or status by the highest authority in the Church, the Roman Pontiff. The opinion therefore which maintains that Greek-Ruthenian confessors in the United States and Canada can absolve any Latin penitent from any censure reserved in the Latin Code except those to which Orientals are subject does not seem tenable (pp. 90-95).

13. Oriental as well as Latin interritual confessors may make use of the extensions of material competence according to the conditions described in canons 882, 935, 990, § 2, 2252, 2254 and 2290 (pp. 95-102).

BIBLIOGRAPHY

Sources

Acta Apostolicae Sedis, Commentarium Officiale, Romae, 1909—

Acta et Decreta Concilii Nationis Armenorum habiti ad Sancti Nicolai Tolentinatis anno MDCCCCXI, Romae: Typis Polyglottis Vaticanis, 1913.

Acta et Decreta Sacrorum Conciliorum Recentiorum, Collectio Lacensis, 7 vols., Friburgi Brisgoviae, 1870-1892.

Acta Sanctae Sedis, 41 vols., Romae, 1865-1908.

Bouscaren, T. Lincoln, *The Canon Law Digest,* 2 vols. and Supplement, Milwaukee: Bruce, 1934, 1943, 1949.

Bullarum Diplomatum et Privilegiorum Sanctorum Romanorum Pontificum Tauriensis Editio, 24 vols. et Appendix, Augustae Taurinorum, 1857-1872.

Bullarium Franciscanum, 9 vols., Vol. I-III, ed. Joannis Sbaraleae, Romae, 1759-1765.

Canones et Decreta Concilii Tridentini, Taurini, 1913.

Codex Iuris Canonici Pii X Pontificis Maximi iussu digestus Benedicti Papae XV auctoritate promulgatus, Romae: Typis Polyglottis Vaticanis, 1917.

Codicis Iuris Canonici Fontes, cura Emi Petri Card. Gasparii editi, 9 vols., Romae (postea Civitate Vaticana): Typis Polyglottis Vaticanis, 1923-1939. (Vols. VII-IX ed. cura et studio Emi Iustiniani Card. Serédi.)

Codificazione Canonica Orientale, Fonti, Serie I, 13 fasc., Serie II, 17 fasc., *Fontes,* Series III, Vols. I, II, VI, Città del Vaticano: Tipografia Poliglotta Vaticana, 1930—

Collectanea S. Congregationis de Propaganda Fide, 2 vols., Romae, 1907.

Corpus Iuris Canonici, ed. Lipsiensis secunda, post Aemilii Richteri curas instruxit Aemilius Friedberg, 2 vols., Lipsiae, 1879-1881.

Corpus Iuris Civilis, 3 vols., Vol. III, *Novellae,* recognovit Rudolfus Schoell, absolvit Gulielmus Kroll, ed. stereotypa quinta, Berolini: Apud Weidmannos, 1928.

Decretales D. Gregorii Papae IX suae integritati una cum glossis restitutae, Romae, 1582.

Decretum Gratiani emendatum et observationibus illustratum una cum glossis, 2 vols., Romae, 1582.

Denzinger, Heinrich-Bannwart, Clemens et Umberg, Johannes, *Enchiridion Symbolorum, Definitionum, et Declarationum de Rebus Fidei et Morum,* 21.-23. ed., Friburgi Brisgoviae: Herder & Co., 1937.

Holoweckyj, Dionysius, *Fontes Iuris Canonici Ecclesiae Ruthenae,* Romae: Typis Polyglottis Vaticanis, 1932.

Jaffé, Phillipus, *Regesta Pontificum Romanorum ab condita Ecclesia ad annum post Christum natum MCXCVIII,* 2. ed., correctam et auctam auspiciis Gulielmi Wattenbach curaverunt F. Kaltenbrunner, P. Ewald, S. Löwenfeld, 2 tomes in 1 vol., Lipsiae, 1885-1888.

Liber Sextus Decretalium D. Bonifacii Papae VIII, suae integritati cum Clementinis et Extravagantibus, earumque Glossis restitutis, Romae, 1582.

Mansi, J. D., *Sacrorum Conciliorum Nova et Amplissima Collectio,* 53 vols. in 60, Parisiis, Arnhem, Lipsiae, 1901-1927.

Monumenta Germaniae Historica, Scriptores Rerum Langobardicarum et Italicarum, Saec. VI-IX, ed. G. Waitz, Hannoverae: Impensis Bibliopolii Hahniani, 1878.

Potthast, Augustus, *Regesta Pontificum Romanorum inde ab anno post Christum natum MCXCVIII ad annum MCCCIV,* 2 vols., Berolini, 1874-1875.

———, *Sacrae Romanae Rotae Sententiae seu Decisiones ab Anno 1909—,* Typis Polyglottis Vaticanis, 1912—

Schroeder, H., *Canons and Decrees of the Council of Trent,* St. Louis: B. Herder & Co., 1941.

Sylloge Praecipuorum Documentorum Recentium Summorum Pontificum et S. Congregationis de Propaganda Fide necnon aliarum SS. Congregationum Romanarum, Romae: Typis Polyglottis Vaticanis, 1939.

Synodus Provincialis Ruthenorum habita in civitate Zamosciae anno MDCCXX, 3. ed., Romae, 1883.

Synodus Sciarfensis Syrorum in Monte Libano celebrata anno 1888, Romae: Typis Polyglottis S. C. de Prop. Fide, 1896.

Reference Works

Aertnys, J.-Damen, C., *Theologia Moralis secundum doctrinam S. Alfonsi,* 15. ed., 2 vols., Romae: Marietti, 1947.

Alphonsus Liguori, St., *Theologia Moralis,* ed. L. Gaudé, 4 vols., Romae, 1905-1912.

Annuario Pontificio per l'anno 1948, Città del Vaticano: Tipographia Poliglotta Vaticana, 1948.

Augustine, Charles, *A Commentary on the New Code of Canon Law,* 8 vols., St. Louis, 1918-1922.

Augustinus, Antonius, *Antiquae Collectiones Decretalium,* Ilerdae, 1576.

Ayrinhac, H. A., *Legislation on the Sacraments in the New Code of Canon Law,* New York-London: Longmans, Green & Co., 1928.

———, *Penal Legislation in the New Code of Canon Law,* New York-Cincinnati-Chicago: Benziger Brothers, 1920.

Ballerini, Antonius-Palmieri, Dominicus, *Opus Theologicum Morale,* 7 vols., Prati, 1889-1893.

Barbosa, Augustinus, *Collectanea Doctorum tam Veterum quam Recentiorum in Ius Pontificium Universum,* 5 vols., Lugduni, 1669.

Baronius, Caesar, *Annales Ecclesiastici,* 37 vols., ed. A. Theiner, Vols. I-XXVIII, Barri-Ducis, 1864-1875; Vols. XXIX-XXXVII, Parisiis, 1876-1897.

Bélanger, Louis, *Les Ukrainiens catholiques du rit grec-ruthène au Canada,* Quebec: l'Université Laval, 1945.

Benedictus XIV, *De Synodo Dioecesana,* 2 vols., Parmae, 1764.

Berger, Élie, *Les Registres d'Innocent IV,* 4 vols., Paris: Fontemoing, 1884-1897.

Bernardus Papiensis, *Summa Decretalium,* ed. E. A. Th. Laspeyres, Ratisbonae, 1860.

Berutti, Christophorus, *Institutiones Iuris Canonici,* 6 vols., Vol. I, *Normae Generales,* 1936; Vol. VI, *De Delictis et Poenis,* 1938, Taurini-Romae: Marietti.

Beste, Udalricus, *Introductio in Codicem,* 2. ed., Collegeville, Minn.: St. John's Abbey Press, 1944.

Billot, L., *Tractatus de Ecclesia Christi,* 2 vols., Vol. I, 5. ed., Romae: Apud Aedes Universitatis Gregorianae, 1927.

———, *De Ecclesiae Sacramentis,* 7. ed., 2 vols., Romae: Apud Aedes Universitatis Gregorianae, 1929-1931.

Blat, Albertus, *Commentarium Textus Codicis Iuris Canonici,* 5 vols. in 6, Romae, 1921-1927; Liber III, Pars I, *De Sacramentis,* 1920; Liber V, *De Delictis et Poenis,* 1924, Romae: Collegio Angelico.

Cappello, Felix M., *Summa Iuris Canonici,* 3 vols., Vol. I, Romae: Apud Aedes Universitatis Gregorianae, 1928.

———, *Tractatus Canonico-Moralis de Censuris,* 2. ed., Taurinorum Augustae: Marietti, 1925.

———, *Tractatus Canonico-Moralis de Sacramentis,* 3 vols. in 6, Vol. II, Pars I, *De Poenitentia,* 3. ed., Taurinorum Augustae: Marietti, 1939; Vol. III, *De Matrimonio,* 2. ed., Taurinorum Augustae: Marietti, 1927.

Christ, Joseph, *Dispensation from Vindicative Penalties,* The Catholic University of America Canon Law Studies, n. 174, Washington, D. C.: The Catholic University of America Press, 1943.

Cicognani, Amleto, *Canon Law,* 2. ed. trans. by J. O'Hara and F. Brennan, Westminster: The Newman Bookshop, 1947.

Ciesluk, Joseph, *National Parishes in the United States,* The Catholic University of America Canon Law Studies, n. 190, Washington, D. C.: The Catholic University of America Press, 1944.

Clancy, Patrick, *The Local Religious Superior,* The Catholic University of America Canon Law Studies, n. 175, Washington, D. C.: The Catholic University of America Press, 1943.

Coronata, Matthaeus Conte a, *De Sacramentis Tractatus Canonicus,* 3 vols., Taurini-Romae: Marietti, 1943-1946.

———, *Institutiones Iuris Canonici,* 2. ed., 5 vols., Taurini-Romae: Marietti, 1939-1947.

Coussa, Acacius, *Epitome Praelectionum de Iure Ecclesiastico Orientali,* 2 vols., Vol. I, Romae: Typis Polyglottis Vaticanis, 1940; Vol. II, Typis Polyglottis Insulae S. Lazari, 1941.

D'Annibale, Josephus, *Summula Theologiae Moralis,* 5. ed., 3 vols., Romae, 1908.

Dargin, Edward, *Reserved Cases According to the Code of Canon Law,* The Catholic University of America Canon Law Studies, n. 20, Washington, D. C.: The Catholic University of America, 1924.

Dausend, Hugo, *Das interrituelle Recht im Codex Iuris Canonici,* Paderborn: Schöningh, 1939.

De Lugo, Ioannes, *Disputationes Scholasticae et Morales,* 2. ed., 8 vols., Parisiis, 1868-1869.

De Meester, A., *Juris Canonici et Juris Canonico-Civilis Compendium,* nova ed., 3 vols. in 4, Brugis, 1921-1928.

Diederichs, Michael, *The Jurisdiction of the Latin Ordinaries over Their Oriental Subjects,* The Catholic University of America Canon Law Studies, n. 229, Washington, D. C.: The Catholic University of America Press, 1946.

Dictionnaire de Théologie Catholique, 15 vols. in 30, Paris: Librairie Letouzey et Ané, 1903—

Duskie, John, *The Canonical Status of the Orientals in the United States,* The Catholic University of America Canon Law Studies, n. 48, Washington, D. C.: The Catholic University of America, 1928

Dziob, Michael, *The Sacred Congregation for the Oriental Church,* The Catholic University of America Canon Law Studies, n. 214, Washington, D. C.: The Catholic University of America Press, 1945.

Eidenschink, John, *The Election of Bishops in the Letters of Pope Gregory the Great,* The Catholic University of America Canon Law Studies, n. 215, Washington, D. C.: The Catholic University of America Press, 1945.

Eubel, C., *Hierarchia Catholica Medii Aevi,* 2. ed., 3 vols., Monasterii, 1913-1935.

Ferraris, Lucius, *Prompta Bibliotheca Canonica, Iuridica, Moralis, Theologica, necnon Ascetica, Polemica, Rubricistica, Historica,* 8 vols., Romae, 1885-1892. Vol. IX, ed. I. Bucceroni, Romae, 1899.

Fortescue, Adrian, *The Uniate Eastern Churches,* ed. G. Smith, New York, 1923.

Gay, Jules, *L'Italie Méridionale et l'Empire Byzantine,* Paris: Fontemoing, 1904.

Gonzalez-Tellez, Emmanuel, *Commentaria Perpetua in Singulos Textus Quinque Librorum Decretalium Gregorii IX,* 5 vols. in 4, Venetiis, 1699.

Graesse, G. Th., *Orbis Latinus,* 2. ed., Berolini, 1909.

Hagedorn, Francis, *General Legislation on Indulgences,* The Catholic University of America Canon Law Studies, n. 22, Washington, D. C.: The Catholic University of America, 1924.

Hefele, Charles-LeClercq, Henri, *Histoire des Conciles,* 10 vols. in 19, Paris: Librairie Letouzey et Ané, 1907-1938.

Hickey, John, *Irregularities and Simple Impediments in the New Code of Canon Law,* The Catholic University of America Canon Law Studies, n. 7, Washington, D. C.: The Catholic University of America, 1920.

Hostiensis, Henricus, *In Libros Decretalium Commentaria,* 5 vols. in 3, Venetiis, 1581.

———, *Summa Aurea,* Venetiis, 1570.

Huber, Raphael, *A Documented History of the Franciscan Order (1182-1517),* Milwaukee, Wis. and Washington, D. C.: The Nowiny Publishing Apostolate, Inc., 1944.

Kearney, Raymond, *The Principles of Delegation,* The Catholic University of America Canon Law Studies, n. 55, Washington, D. C.: The Catholic University of America, 1929.

Kelly, James, *The Jurisdiction of the Confessor,* New York, Cincinnati, Chicago: Benziger Brothers, 1929.

Marbach, Joseph, *Marriage Legislation for the Catholics of the Oriental Rites in the United States and Canada,* The Catholic University of America Canon Law Studies, n. 243, Washington, D. C.: The Catholic University of America Press, 1946.

Maroto, Philippus, *Institutiones Iuris Canonici,* 2 vols., Vol. I, 3. ed., Romae, 1921.

McCormick, Robert, *Confessors of Religious,* The Catholic University of America Canon Law Studies, n. 33, Washington, D. C.: The Catholic University of America, 1926.

Michiels, G., *De Delictis et Poenis,* Vol. I, *De Delictis,* Lublin-Polonia: Universitas Catholica, 1934.

———, *Normae Generales Iuris Canonici, Commentarium Libri I Codicis Iuris Canonici,* 2 vols., Lublin, 1929.

Migne, Jacques Paul, *Patrologiae Cursus Completus—Series Graeca,* 161 vols., Parisiis, 1856-1866.

———, *Patrologiae Cursus Completus,—Series Latina,* 221 vols., Parisiis, 1844-1864.

Moriarity, Francis, *The Extraordinary Absolution from Censures,* The Catholic University of America Canon Law Studies, n. 113, Washington, D. C.: The Catholic University of America, 1938.

Motry, Hubert, *Diocesan Faculties According to the Code of Canon Law,* The Catholic University of America Canon Law Studies, n. 16, Washington, D. C.: The Catholic University of America, 1922.

Noldin, H.-Schmitt, A., *Summa Theologiae Moralis iuxta Codicem Iuris Canonici,* 26. ed., 3 vols., Oeniponte-Lipsiae: Rauch, 1939.

Ottaviani, Alaphridus, *Institutiones Iuris Publici Ecclesiastici,* 2 vols. in 1, Romae: Apud Aedes Facultatis Iuridicae ad S. Apollinaris, 1925.

Pallavicini, Sfortia, *Vera Concilii Tridentini Historia,* 3 vols., Antverpiae, 1670.

Pallen, Condé B., *A Memorial of Andrew J. Shipman, His Life and Writings,* New York: Encyclopedia Press, Inc., 1916.

Petra, Vincentius, *Commentaria in Constitutiones Apostolicas,* 5 vols. in 2, Venetiis, 1729.

Petrani, Alexius, *De Relatione Iuridica inter Diversos Ritus in Ecclesia Catholica,* Taurini et Romae: Marietti, 1930.

Pirhing, E., *Ius Canonicum,* 5 vols., Dilingae, 1674-1678.

Prümmer, Dominicus, *Manuale Theologiae Moralis,* 8. ed., 3 vols., Friburgi Brisgoviae: Herder & Co., 1935-1936.

Quigley, Joseph, *Condemned Societies,* The Catholic University of America Canon Law Studies, n. 46, Washington, D. C.: The Catholic University of America, 1927.

Reiffenstuel, Anacletus, *Ius Canonicum Universum,* ed. R. D. Victoris Pelletier, 7 vols., Parisiis, 1864-1870.

Rodrigo, Lucius, *Praelectiones Theologico-Moralis Comillensis,* Series I, *Theologia Moralis Fundamentalis,* Tom. II, *Tractatus de Legibus,* Santander: Sal Terrae, 1944.

Ryan, Gerald, *Principles of Episcopal Jurisdiction,* The Catholic University of America Canon Law Studies, n. 120, Washington, D. C.: The Catholic University of America Press, 1939.

Sabetti, A.-Barrett, T., *Compendium Theologiae Moralis,* 30. ed., New York: Pustet, 1924.

Schroeder, H. J., *Disciplinary Decrees of the General Councils,* St. Louis: B. Herder Book Co., 1937.

Shuhler, Ralph, *Privileges of Regulars to Absolve and Dispense,* The Catholic University of America Canon Law Studies, n. 186, Washington, D. C.: The Catholic University of America Press, 1943.

Stadalnikas, Casimir, *Reservation of Censures,* The Catholic University of America Canon Law Studies, n. 208, Washington, D. C.: The Catholic University of America Press, 1944.

Statistica con cenni storici della Gerarchia e dei Fedeli di Rito Orientale, Sacra Congregazione Orientale, Roma: Typografia Poliglotta Vaticana, 1932.

The Official Catholic Directory, 1949, New York: P. J. Kenedy & Sons, 1949.

Thomas Aquinas, St., *Summa Theologica,* 6 vols., Taurini: Marietti, 1937.

Thomassinus, Ludovicus, *Vetus et Nova Ecclesiae Disciplina circa Beneficia et Beneficiarios,* 10 vols., Magontiaci, 1787.

Van Espen, Z. Bernardus, *Ius Ecclesiasticum Universum,* 5 vols., Lovanii, 1778.

Van Hove, A., *Commentarium Lovaniense in Codicem Iuris Canonici,* Vol. I, Tom. II, *De Legibus Ecclesiasticis,* Mechliniae-Romae: H. Dessain, 1930.

Vermeersch, Arturus-Creusen, Josephus, *Epitome Iuris Canonici,* 3 vols., Vol. I, 6. ed., 1937; Vol. II, 6. ed., 1940; Vol. III, 5. ed., 1936, Mechliniae-Romae: H. Dessain.

Wadding, Luke, *Annales Minores,* 3. ed., 27 vols., Quaracchi, 1931-1934.

Wernz, F. X., *Ius Decretalium,* 6 vols., Vols. I-IV, 2. ed., Romae et Prati, 1905-1912.

Woywod, Stanislaus-Smith, Callistus, *A Practical Commentary on the Code of Canon Law,* 2 vols., New York: Joseph F. Wagner, Inc., 1948.

Watkins, O., *A History of Penance,* 2 vols., London: Longmans, Green & Co., 1920.

Zitelli-Natali, Zephyrinus, *Apparatus Iuris Ecclesiastici,* Romae, 1886.

Articles

Herman, E., "De 'Ritu' in Iure Canonico," *Orientalia Christiana,* XXXII (1933), 96-158.

Meehan, A. B., "The Greek Ruthenian Church in the United States," *The Ecclesiastical Review,* LI (1914), 710-717.

Plöchl, Willibald, "The Fundamental Principles of the Philosophy of Canon Law," *The Jurist,* IV (1944), 70-100.

Vermeersch, A., "De Indulgentiis quoad Fideles Ritus Orientalis," *Periodica de Re Canonica et Morali,* IX (1920), 67-68.

Willis, C. J., "*Ius Clavium* iuxta Sanctum Thomam," *The Jurist,* I (1941), 108-124.

Periodicals

American Ecclesiastical Review, The, Vols. I-XXXII, Philadelphia, 1889-1905; from 1905: *The Ecclesiastical Review,* Vols. XXXIII-CIX, Philadelphia, 1905-1943; from 1944: *The American Ecclesiastical Review,* Washington, D. C., Vol. CX, 1944—

Analecta Iuris Pontificii, Romae, 1855-1869; Parisiis, 1872-1891.

Apollinaris, Romae, 1928—

Canoniste Contemporain, Le, 45 vols., Paris, 1878-1922.

Eparkhialne Visti, Philadelphia, 1926—

Jurist, The, Washington, D. C., 1941—

Orientalia Christiana, Romae, 1922-1935; ab anno 1935: *Orientalia Christiana Analecta,* Romae, 1935—

Periodica de Religiosis et Missionariis, 8 vols., Brugis, 1905-1919; from 1920: *Periodica de Re Canonica et Morali utilia praesertim Religiosis et Missionariis,* 7 vols., Brugis, 1920-1927; from 1927: *Periodica de Re Morali, Canonica, Liturgica,* Brugis (1927-1936) et Romae, 1937—

Theological Studies, Woodstock, Md., 1940—

ABBREVIATIONS

AAS—*Acta Apostolicae Sedis.*
AER—*The American Ecclesiastical Review.*
ASS—*Acta Sanctae Sedis.*
Bull. Franc.—*Bullarium Franciscanum Romanorum Pontificum Constitutiones, Epistolas ac Diplomata Continens.*
Bull. Rom.—*Bullarum Diplomatum . . . Tauriensis Editio.*
Coll. Lac.—*Collectio Lacensis.*
Coll. S.C.P.F.—*Collectanea S. Congregationis de Propaganda Fide.*
DB.—Denzinger-Bannwart-Umberg, *Enchiridion Symbolorum . . .*
Fontes—*Codicis Iuris Canonici Fontes.*
Fonti—*Codificazione Canonica Orientale, Fonti.*
Mansi—*Sacrorum Conciliorum Nova et Amplissima Collectio.*
PCI—Pontificia Commissio Interpretationis Codicis.
Potthast—*Regesta Pontificum Romanorum . . .*
S.C.C.—Sacra Congregatio Concilii.
S. C. de Prop. Fide—Sacra Congregatio de Propaganda Fide.
S. C. Or.—Sacra Congregatio pro Ecclesia Orientali.
S. C. S. Off.—Suprema Congregatio Sancti Officii.

ALPHABETICAL INDEX

Absolution, sacramental,
  nature of, 28-29
Alphonsus, St.,
  and jurisdiction over *peregrini*, 37-38
Annual confession,
  law of IV Lateran Council on, 18-22
Apostolic Constitutions,
  inclusion of Orientals in, 77-82
Approbati,
  its meaning in canon 881, § 1, 40

Benedict XIV, Pope,
  and Orientals in Constitutions, 78
Bishops, confessors of, 64-65
  interritual rights of, 68-69

Canon 1,
  and interritual right of penitent, 32
  and Oriental confessor's power to absolve, 90-95
  and subjection of Orientals to the reservations of the Latin Church, 77-84.
Canon 881, § 1
  and confessors of Oriental rites, 36-37
  and jurisdiction over travelers, 37-40
  meaning of *approbati* in, 40
  purpose of, 36
Canons penitentiary,
  jurisdiction of,
    local, 42
    personal, 56
Cardinals,
  confessors of, 64-65
  interritual right of, 68-69
  personal jurisdiction of, 55-59

Causae maiores, 6
Censure,
  nature of a, 72
  reserved,
    effect on power to absolve, 72-73
    by Holy See,
      Oriental confessor's jurisdiction over one certainly incurred by Latin penitent, 91-95
      to which Orientals are subject, 76-84
    by local ordinaries in U. S. and Canada,
      interritual law concerning, 84-90
    extraordinary power to absolve, 95-99
    subjection to,
      Latins, 74-75
      Orientals, 75-84
Chaplains, military,
  jurisdiction of, 55-59
Clerics of Oriental rites,
  regulations of the Holy See and,
    non-Ruthenians, 45-48
    Ruthenians, 49-50
Commutation of works prescribed for the gaining of indulgences, 95-99
Competence of the interritual confessor,
  material,
    limitations of, 71-95
    extensions of, 95-102
  with local jurisdiction,
    his local, 42-52
    his personal, 35-42, 48, 52
  with personal jurisdiction,
    ordinary, 55-59
    delegated, 59-63
    derived *a iure*, 63-69

Concession of confessional jurisdiction,
 and ordinaries,
  of Latin rite, 44-48, 59-63
  of Ruthenian rite, 48-51, 59-63
Confessor, interritual rights of, 28-31
Constitution *Apostolicae Sedis,*
 and Orientals, 79

Delegation of confessional jurisdiction,
 local, 44-51
 personal, 59-63

Exarchates, the Ruthenian,
 their erection in U. S. and Canada, 12-15
  effects of, 15-16
Exarchs, the Ruthenian Apostolic,
 nature of their jurisdiction, 14-16

Form of Marriage,
 extraordinary power to dispense from, 95-99
Freedom, the interritual,
 of the confessor, 28-31
 of the penitent, 31-34

Interritual confessor,
 definition of an, VII
 competence of, cf. Competence
 jurisdiction of, cf. Jurisdiction
Irregularities,
 confessor's extraordinary power to dispense from, 95-102
Italo-Greek rite, confessors of, 27, 36

Jurisdiction,
 in general,
  nature of, 1-2
  kinds of, 3-4
  of Roman Pontiff, 5-6
  episcopal, 6-9
  of Patriarchs, 9
 in the United States and Canada,
  personal-territorial of the Ruthenian ordinaries, 14-16
  territorial of Latin ordinaries, 10-11, 14-16
 of the internal sacramental forum, 2-3
  local,
   subject to Latin ordinaries,
    Latin confessors with, 42-45
    Oriental confessors with, 45-48
   subject to Ruthenian ordinaries,
    confessors with, 48-52
   personal extent of, 35-37
   special restrictions on, 40-42, 44, 48, 52
  personal,
   confessors with,
    ordinary, 55-59
    delegated, 59-63
    derived *a iure,* 63-69
   differs from local, 53-54
Language and rite,
 the care of the faithful of different,
  legislation of IV Lateran Council on, 17-21
  in the United States and Canada,
   non-Ruthenians, 10-12
   Ruthenians, 12-16
Latin churches and oratories,
 the exercise of Ruthenian confessional jurisdiction in,
  local, 40-42, 52
  personal, 57-58
Local ordinaries,
 confessional jurisdiction of,
  local, 39, 42-45, 48-52
  personal, 39, 53-59, 63-69

Masonic sects, penalties against,
 and Orientals,
  prior to the Code, 79
  mitigations in the Code, 80-83
Material competence, cf. Competence
Matrimonial impediments,
 extraordinary power to dispense, 95-99

Occasional confessor of women religious, 67-69
Offices, jurisdictional,
of divine origin, 4-7
of ecclesiastical origin, 7-8
Ordinaries, cf. Local ordinaries
Oriental rites in the U. S. and Canada,
members of the,
jurisdiction over,
non-Ruthenians, 11-12, 15
Ruthenians, 12-16
their subjection to reservations,
in law of the rite, 75
in law of the territory, 76
in law of the Code, 76-84
clerics of,
regulations of the Holy See and, 11-12, 44-51

Pastors, confessional jurisdiction of,
local, 42-45
personal, 55-59
Patriarchs, jurisdiction of, 9
Penitent,
the interritual right of the, 31-33
the relation between confessor and, 29-30
Peregrini,
local confessor's jurisdiction and, 37-40
Periodeutae, 9
Privileges, confessional,
of bishops and cardinals, 64-65, 68-69
of religious Orders, 22-25
of women religious, 65-69
Religious,
papal confessional privileges of,
Boniface VIII and, 22-23
interritual administration of the sacrament of penance and, 23-25
superiors of exempt clerical institutes of,
confessional jurisdiction of, 56
delegation of, 59-63
local and personal extent of, 56-57
Reservations,
and penitents of
Latin rite, 74-75
Oriental rites, 74-84
extraordinary power to absolve, 95-99
interritual confessor and those of,
Holy See, 90-95
local ordinarics, 84-90
nature and kinds of, 71-74
Rite, the Greek-Ruthenian,
churches and oratories of,
jurisdiction over, 16, 48-49
exercise of local confessional jurisdiction in, 40-42, 44, 48, 52
exarchates of, cf. Exarchates
ordinaries of,
competence of confessors with local jurisdiction from, 49-52
confessional jurisdiction of,
local, 48-52
personal, 57-58
their jurisdiction in general, 14-16
rectors of churches or missions of,
confessional jurisdiction of,
local, 50-52
personal, 57-58

Sacrament of penance,
the requisites in the minister of, 28-29
Sin,
the confessor's power to absolve from, 71-72
the reservation of,
its nature, 71-73
kinds of, 74

reserved by the Holy See,
and penitents,
of the Latin rite, 75-76
of the Oriental rites, 76-84
and power of confessor to absolve,
extensions of, 89, 95-99
limitations on, 90-95
reserved by local ordinaries,
and interritual confessors,
special law concerning, 84-90
and penitents
of Latin rite, 74-75
of Oriental rites, 75-76

Vindictive penalties,
and interritual confessor's power to dispense from, 95-102
Women religious,
confessional jurisdiction over,
ordinary, 55
delegated, 61
confessor of,
occasional, 67-68
seriously ill, 65-66
interritual confessional privileges of, 68-69

BIOGRAPHICAL NOTE

JOHN J. WALSH was born on July 30, 1913, in Philadelphia, Pennsylvania. He received his primary education at the parochial schools of St. Columba and Our Lady of the Holy Souls in the same city. After one year at Northeast Catholic High School in that city, he entered the Holy Ghost Missionary College, Cornwells Heights, Pennsylvania. In 1933 he was admitted to the novitiate of the Holy Ghost Fathers at Ridgefield, Connecticut, where he made his religious profession on July 31, 1934. The same year he began his philosophical studies at the Holy Ghost Mission Seminary, Ferndale, Norwalk, Connecticut, and received the degree of Bachelor of Arts in 1936. At the end of the first year of theology at the same Seminary, he enrolled in the School of Sacred Theology of the University of Fribourg, Switzerland, where he received the degree of Bachelor of Theology in June, 1939. He was elevated to the sacred priesthood on July 23, 1939. Forced by the outbreak of World War II to return to the United States, he completed his theological studies at the Holy Ghost Mission Seminary. In 1940 he was appointed assistant at the Church of St. Mark the Evangelist, New York. Five years later he was admitted to the School of Canon Law of the Catholic University of America. In June, 1946, he received the Baccalaureate in Canon Law, and in June, 1947, the Licentiate in Canon Law.

CANON LAW STUDIES *

306. Waters, Rev. Joseph L., S.S.J., J.C.L., The Probation in Societies ot Quasi-Religious.

307. Regan, Rev. Michael J., J.C.L., Canon 16.

308. Byrne, Rev. Harry J., J.C.L., Investment of Church Funds.

309. Gallagher, Rev. Thomas V., J.C.L., The Rejection of Judicial Witnesses and Testimony.

310. Chatham, Rev. Josiah G., Ph.D., S.T.L., J.C.L., Force and Fear as Invalidating Marriage: The Element of Injustice.

311. Brown, Rev. James Victor, O.R.S.A., J.C.L., The Invalidating Effects of Force, Fear, and Fraud upon the Canonical Novitiate.

312. Duerr, Rev. Charles J., B.A., J.C.L., The Judicial Notary.

313. Gonzalez, Rev. Francisco J., O.S.A., J.C.L., De Parocho Religioso Eiusque Superiore Locali.

314. Hannon, Rev. James J., J.C.L., Holy Viaticum.

315. Sadlowski, Rev. Edwin L., J.C.L., The Sacred Furnishings of Churches.

316. Sego, Rev. Arthur A., J.C.L., Dispensation from the Interpellations.

317. Waterhouse, Rev. John M., J.C.L., The Power of the Local Ordinary to Impose a Matrimonial Ban.

318. Frein, Rev. Eugene B., J.C.L., The Discretionary Power of the Defender of the Matrimonial Bond.

319. Carton, Rev. George A., J.C.L., The Time Factor in the Gaining of Indulgences.

320. Walsh, Rev. John J., C.S.Sp., J.C.L., The Jurisdiction of the Interritual Confessor in the United States and Canada.

321. Unterkoefler, Rev. Ernest L., S.T.L., J.C.L., The Presiding Judge in Matrimonial Causes of First Instance.

---

* A complete list of the available numbers in the series will be found in earlier studies. Send orders to: The Catholic University of America Press, 620 Michigan Ave., N.E., Washington 17, D. C.

www.ingramcontent.com/pod-product-compliance
Lightning Source LLC
LaVergne TN
LVHW050205080826
844660LV00012B/356

* 9 7 8 0 8 1 3 2 2 4 9 3 0 *